The Collected Works of
James M. Buchanan

VOLUME 2

Public Principles of Public Debt

James M. Buchanan

The Collected Works of

James M. Buchanan

VOLUME 2

Public Principles of Public Debt

A Defense and Restatement

LIBERTY FUND

Indianapolis

This book is published by Liberty Fund, Inc., a foundation
established to encourage study of the ideal of a society of free
and responsible individuals.

𒀝𒆤 𒄊𒂼

The cuneiform inscription that serves as our logo and as the design
motif for our endpapers is the earliest-known written appearance
of the word "freedom" (*amagi*), or "liberty." It is taken from a clay
document written about 2300 B.C. in the Sumerian city-state of Lagash.

First published in 1958 by Richard D. Irwin, Inc.

03	02	01			C	5	4	3	2	
03	02	01	00	99	P	5	4	3	2	1

Library of Congress Cataloging-in-Publication Data
Buchanan, James M.
Public principles of public debt.
p.   cm. — (The collected works of James M. Buchanan ; v. 2)
Includes bibliographical references and index.
ISBN 0-86597-215-x (alk. paper). — ISBN 0-86597-216-8 (pbk. : alk. paper)
1. Debts, Public.   I. Title.   II. Series: Buchanan, James M.
Works.   1999 ; v. 2.
HJ8015.B8   1999
336.3'4—dc21   98-45533

LIBERTY FUND, INC.
8335 Allison Pointe Trail, Suite 300
Indianapolis, IN 46250-1684

"I find little use for the hypothesis that error becomes truth merely by long or consistent practice."

—Henry Simons, "On Debt Policy"

"I must confess, that there is a strange supineness, from long custom, creeped into all ranks of men, with regard to public debts, not unlike what divines so vehemently complain of with regard to their religious doctrines."

—David Hume, "Of Public Credit"

Contents

Foreword

Begin with a picture. Here is the young Jim Buchanan, strolling down the stairs of the Hotel d'Inghilterra in Rome after breakfast in early 1957. He is preoccupied. His brow is slightly furrowed. Suddenly, he looks up, and his head tilts back. A slightly incredulous look comes over his face. Apparently, something puzzling had in an instant become clear. He races down the remaining steps and hurries over to a small writing room that graces the foyer of the hotel. Grabbing some pieces of hotel stationery, he proceeds feverishly to jot down the crucial points. *Public Principles of Public Debt*[1] is born.

It is, for Buchanan, the only book that will come about in this way—as a flash of inspiration. Other works may be no less inspired in an intellectual sense—and no less inspiring to readers. But *Public Principles of Public Debt* is the only work that will begin with an experience of quite this Road-to-Damascus quality. And the feverishness does not end here. The central point of the argument, once seen, is so obvious to Buchanan—the prevailing orthodoxy on public debt incidence (which he had previously thoroughly imbibed) so clearly wrong—that he cannot wait to get the book written and into print. As he presses forward with the writing, he anxiously examines the journals, fearful that with so obvious a point he might well be scooped. The natural impulse of intellectual excitement works together here with considerations of professional prudence to drive him on.

Was he right to be anxious? To judge by the book's puzzled reception and the confused literature about it that emerged over the ensuing decade, probably not. What was obvious to Buchanan was clearly not so obvious to everyone else. Indeed, there remained a constituency, particularly within mac-

---

1. James M. Buchanan, *Public Principles of Public Debt: A Defense and Restatement* (Homewood, Ill.: Richard D. Irwin, 1958), volume 2 in the series.

roeconomics, that was staunchly resistant to and suspicious of the Buchanan insights. Nonetheless, Buchanan was right to feel that much was at stake, both professionally and academically; *Public Principles of Public Debt* was, after all, Buchanan's first monograph. And in this sense, it added a depth and substance to his vita to set alongside the impressive array of important journal articles he had already produced. Moreover, the line of argument had important influences on his subsequent work. For example, the subjective cost theme in *Cost and Choice*[2] owes much to the reflections about cost that are developed in *Public Principles of Public Debt,* and the important public choice implications of the *Public Principles of Public Debt* argument surface explicitly in *Democracy in Deficit.*[3]

To elaborate, part of the concern of the "new orthodoxy" in claiming that the burden of debt (at least, internal debt) is borne currently, in the period that the expenditure is undertaken and precisely *not* passed forward to future generations as (allegedly mistaken) popular view might have it, was to offset ethical inhibitions about deficit financing. If Buchanan's claim was right, and the burden of debt financing was indeed borne by "future generations," then debt financing might well encourage both excessive reliance on debt and excessive levels of spending. To the extent that the future generations in question were indeed different persons, not alive (or not enfranchised) at the time the expenditure operation was undertaken, then the fiscal operation would not (and by definition *could* not) fulfill the Wicksellian contractarian requirement that virtually all affected parties should be free to reject the expenditure. In the absence of a restriction on debt financing, ordinary democratic processes could not prevent the current generation of voters-taxpayers from passing forward the cost of as much current expenditure as they were inclined to and—if the cost was to be borne by others—voting for themselves projects whose total benefits, though positive, did not exceed total costs. These aspects remain entirely in the background in *Public Principles of Public Debt.* The object in this first book by Buchanan is to establish a set of analytic claims about debt incidence. But the public choice aspects do pro-

---

2. James M. Buchanan, *Cost and Choice: An Inquiry in Economic Theory* (Chicago: Markham Publishing Co., 1969), volume 6 in the series.

3. James M. Buchanan and Richard E. Wagner, *Democracy in Deficit: The Political Legacy of Lord Keynes* (New York: Academic Press, 1977), volume 8 in the series.

vide some of the (possibly unconscious) subtext in *Public Principles of Public Debt* that Buchanan and Wagner, in *Democracy in Deficit* and elsewhere, make explicit and develop in a more complete way.

These public choice anxieties are, of course, very much in play in the more recent debate over implicit social security debt. This latter debate has, in fact, proceeded somewhat independently of the Buchanan book and has focused on slightly different aspects of the whole issue. In particular, it has been mainly concerned with the question of the effects of debt financing on the capital stock. The classic papers here revolve around the rival claims of Martin S. Feldstein and Robert J. Barro—the former claiming to establish econometrically the empirical magnitude of the effects of social security arrangements on the United States capital stock, the latter purporting to show (through a reinvention of the so-called Ricardian equivalence theorem) that, for fully rational individuals, public debt will have virtually the same effect as taxation.[4] It is an interesting twist here that Barro's agenda is in part an anti-Keynesian one. In 1958, the Keynesian position was that (internal) debt and tax financing were more or less equivalent—at least in the intertemporal allocation of burdens. By 1974, however, the Keynesian position seemed entirely reversed. It was, by 1974, recognized that if taxes and debt were essentially equivalent, then standard macroeconomic policy measures based on deficit management could have no effect on the economy—macroeconomic or otherwise. In fact, the Barro-Feldstein debate—or the debate that might have been—got somewhat sidetracked because of problems with the replicability of Feldstein's data. However, it should be clear that neither Barro's conclusions nor his approach would be particularly congenial to Buchanan. It is essential to Buchanan's argument that debt financing has an effect: the difference between Buchanan and the Keynesians was rather whether such effects were desirable or not. More to the point, perhaps, Barro's central question (and the title of his influential paper)—"are government bonds net wealth?"—is set at a more aggregative level than Buchanan's analysis in *Public Principles of Public Debt*. Indeed, in an important sense, the basic contri-

---

4. Martin S. Feldstein, "Social Security, Induced Retirement, and Aggregate Capital Accumulation," *Journal of Political Economy* 5 (September–October 1974): 905–26; Robert J. Barro, "Are Government Bonds Net Wealth?" *Journal of Political Economy* 6 (November–December 1974): 1095–117.

bution in *Public Principles of Public Debt* is Buchanan's insistence on an appropriately disaggregated, individuated mode of analysis. To the standard new orthodox claim that we owe internal debt to ourselves, Buchanan's response is effectively: What's this "we" business? Once it is recognized that incidence analysis depends on isolating which individuals in which capacities face a liability as a result of a fiscal operation, claims about the community as a whole are seen to be essentially irrelevant and potentially misleading.

It is, of course, not necessary here to repeat Buchanan's argument. That is elegantly and clearly set out in the ensuing text. But, it is worth noting that there is a kind of intellectual divide between those who conceive social phenomena in a disaggregated way and those of a more holistic, organic cast of mind. Arguably, it is this intellectual divide that most distinguishes micro- from macroeconomists and *a fortiori* economists as a group from sociologists and many traditional political theorists. Within this divide, in *Public Principles of Public Debt,* Buchanan establishes himself firmly as an arch exponent of the individualist method.

The years immediately following the publication of Buchanan's book gave rise to an extensive literature, the most important elements of which are reproduced in James M. Ferguson's book, *Public Debt and Future Generations.*[5] Unsurprisingly, public debt has been a recurrent theme in Buchanan's writings over his entire career. And in the more recent resurgence of interest in the topic surrounding the analysis of social security policy, Buchanan has had occasion to revisit earlier themes. What is perhaps surprising, given the change in intellectual climate since the heyday of the new orthodoxy and the overwhelming predominance of Keynesian thinking throughout the fifties and sixties, is how fresh and relevant *Public Principles of Public Debt* remains. To be sure, some minor pieces of the book (most notably the appendix) are somewhat dated and have been included in the present version largely for

---

5. James M. Ferguson, ed., *Public Debt and Future Generations* (Chapel Hill: University of North Carolina Press, 1964). The Buchanan contribution written specifically for the Ferguson collection, "Public Debt, Cost Theory, and the Fiscal Illusion," 150–63, is reproduced in the Collected Works in volume 1, *The Logical Foundations of Constitutional Liberty.* Another Buchanan paper reprinted in the Ferguson volume, " 'La Scienza delle finanze': The Italian Tradition in Fiscal Theory," in *Fiscal Theory and Political Economy: Selected Essays* (Chapel Hill: University of North Carolina Press, 1960), 47–54, is reproduced in the series in volume 15, *Externalities and Public Expenditure Theory,* along with Buchanan's other articles on public debt.

reasons of completeness. But these aspects are minor and do not detract (or *dis*tract) from the power and sweep of the central argument. In fact, *Public Principles of Public Debt* remains one of Buchanan's most important and influential books. The force of this observation is hardly diminished by the observation that some of this influence is revealed in Buchanan's own subsequent writings.

Geoffrey Brennan
Australian National University
1998

Preface

Under what conditions is a book conceived? If we knew, I suspect that we could predict with reasonable accuracy the characteristics of the progeny. The pedestrian parade of factual detail which often epitomizes the published doctoral dissertation reflects the forced mating of reluctant author and uninspiring material. The smashing of straw men suggests the rapacious advance of a zealous author determined to defeat his opposition rather than to provide enlightenment.

Because it seems likely that I shall be placed in the second of these categories by some of my professional colleagues, let me explain in some detail just how this little book has come to be written. First of all, I should state that for many years I have accepted what I have called in this book the "new orthodoxy" of the public debt. In my study I have absorbed this doctrine uncritically; in my teaching, I have encouraged others to do the same. If there is no evidence of the "new orthodoxy" in my published papers, this reflects a full and unquestioning integration of the doctrine in my own thinking rather than the reverse.

One great value of considering practical questions of public policy or "political economy" is that the economist is forced to question the validity of so many of the basic elements in his conceptual scheme of things. My re-examination of public debt theory stems directly from my work on a currently important issue in political economy, the national highway problem. In the academic year, 1954–1955, I started working on a manuscript, which remains incomplete, of a book on economic policy in this area of emerging national importance. In the first draft I reached a point at which an appropriate chapter on "Taxes versus Loans" should have appeared. At about this same time, in the spring of 1955, I was serving as a consultant for the Committee for Economic Development. The Committee was attempting to formulate a policy statement on highway modernization, and especially on the methods of financing highway improvement. (The Committee's views are published in the policy statement, *Modernizing the Nation's Highways,* issued in January, 1956.) Central to the highway problem was, and is, the issue of pay-as-we-go versus go-as-we-pay. The Presidential Advisory Committee, under the chairmanship of General Lucius Clay, had proposed a vast new issue of special bonds to finance an accelerated development of an interstate highway network. This financing scheme was given the now-famous luke-warm treatment by the then Secretary of the Treasury Humphrey, and the proposal aroused bitter congressional and public opposition. What was the desirable means of financing highway improvement, admitted to be needed by almost all parties to the discussion? Should taxes be increased sufficiently to cover the full current outlay from currently collected funds, or should public borrowing be accepted as an appropriate means of financing? Surely here was a problem upon which professionally trained economists should be able to shed some light.

Two things became clear very quickly. First, economists seemed to be able to contribute surprisingly little to the solution of this problem, and, sec-ondly, what little they could contribute was based on a "dusting off" and a utilization of "public" or "classical" views on public debt theory and policy. The conception of the public debt which has achieved dominance among economists during the last twenty years and which characterizes economic thought today was useless in the full-employment world of the 1950's. The chapter on "Taxes versus Loans" remained unwritten. The Highway Revenue Act of 1956 was passed, which incorporated the pay-as-we-go principle of fi-nancing, largely reflecting the "vulgar" or "man-on-the-street" opinions about public debt creation.

During the academic year 1955–1956, I was awarded a Fulbright Research Scholarship for study in Italy. In the course of this work I found that the Ital-ian fiscal theorists have devoted a great deal of attention to the Ricardian proposition that taxes and loans exert identical effects upon an economy. This proposition was debated fully in the works of the classical Italian schol-ars in public finance: Pantaleoni, De Viti De Marco, Griziotti, and Einaudi. In a year largely devoted to reading widely in a foreign language it is ex-tremely difficult to isolate those particular works which specifically affect and modify one's thinking. But I now believe that an approach to public debt theory employed by Pantaleoni, despite the fact that his conclusions were erroneous, led me first to question a single bulwark of the "new orthodoxy," namely the sharp conceptual distinction which it makes between the internal and the external debt. This initial questioning was further motivated by a later reading of some of Einaudi's works. In a specific sense none of the Italian theorists appears to have formulated a fully acceptable theory of public debt and, indeed, the dominant theory in Italy, even prior to the 1930's, has much in common with that which characterizes the "new economics." But the Italian approach to the whole problem of public debt was instrumental in shaping my views as they now stand, and I should, therefore, acknowledge this influence.

Stimulated indirectly by the work of Pantaleoni, I prepared a note on the distinction between the internal and the external public debt in which I tried to show that the currently accepted views must be modified. A version of this note appeared in the *American Economic Review* for December, 1957. A somewhat different version appears as Chapter 6 of this book, and I gratefully acknowledge permission of the editors in allowing me to reprint those portions of the argument which are identical. So firmly anchored in my own thinking were the other two bulwarks of the new orthodoxy that, even in writing the early versions of this critical note, I accepted these two without question. The note was completed in early 1957, after which I returned to the highway manuscript with a view toward finally writing the chapter on "Taxes versus Loans." It was only in the process of writing this chapter that I came to the full realization that the two remaining bulwarks of the "new orthodoxy" are also untenable. I came to realize that the analogy between the public economy and the private economy is applicable to most of the problems of the public debt and that public debt creation does involve a shifting of the real burden to future generations of taxpayers.

Somewhat to my surprise, therefore, I now find myself in the camp of the much-maligned man on the street, the holder of the allegedly vulgar and unsophisticated ideas about the public finances. This heresy places upon me a somewhat greater obligation to spell out the ideas involved in my proposed overthrow of the ruling orthodoxy carefully and precisely. In the chapters which follow I shall not be tilting at windmills nor shall I be attacking straw men. I hope that economists will accept my discussion of the ruling theory of public debt as a fair one. I shall try to show the weaknesses in the orthodox approach and to suggest an alternative one.

The discussion will contain little that is completely new or different. Many parts of it will be readily accepted by those who have been instrumental in shaping the "new orthodoxy" in its current form. Some elements of the argument are to be found in the qualifications which the more careful expositors have used to frame their analyses. And almost all of the ideas developed in this book may be found in "classical" public debt theory. The book will essentially re-establish this theory as the general one. Traces of this "correct" theory are to be found alongside traces of the opposing views throughout the history of the subject.

It is understandable that the now-prevalent theory only gained and held its position of dominance in the decade of the 1930's and its aftermath, the 1940's, although the theory had, of course, been advanced frequently during earlier periods. The approach was directly tied to, and indeed could scarcely have been divorced from, the "new economics." But just as other elements of the "new economics" have been found wanting in the 1950's, so with the public debt theory which it espouses. The time for a shift in emphasis, a synthesis, has arrived.

The book will be limited to a discussion of principles. There would be little usefulness in parading factual details which are either familiar or readily available to the reader, the recounting of which would represent a chore for the writer and a cost to the publisher. I shall first describe the new orthodoxy. Following a brief methodological chapter, I shall then examine each of the three basic propositions of the new orthodoxy. I shall then review the pre-Keynesian literature. This will be followed by an extension of the analysis to the nonclassical cases of depression, war, and inflation. Only in the latter part of the book will I face the issue of "taxes versus loans," and, finally, I shall examine the question of debt retirement. Following the main text there is an Appendix which suggests a conceptual revaluation of the national debt. This Appendix represents an application of the theory developed in the book to the measurement problem. The analysis of the Appendix should be considered exploratory rather than definitive, and the nonspecialist reader may omit the entire Appendix without damage to his understanding of the essential argument of the book.

Colleagues have been helpful in two ways. First, they have made valuable critical comments on earlier drafts of the manuscript, comments which have caused me to remove errors, to modify style, and to shift emphasis. But perhaps more importantly, they have encouraged me to proceed with the publishing of this little book, to believe that its belaboring of a few basic notions may serve some useful purpose. Among these colleagues I should especially mention: Marshall R. Colberg, G. Warren Nutter, James R. Schlesinger, Tipton R. Snaveley, and Leland B. Yeager.

The Institute for Research in the Social Sciences of the University of Virginia provided me with financial aid during the summer of 1957 when the basic writing of the book was completed. In the final putting of black on white, I am indebted to Mrs. Gladys Batson, who typed the manuscript, and to my wife, who has provided editorial assistance. For Mrs. Batson's services, I am indebted to the recently established Thomas Jefferson Center for Studies in Political Economy of the University of Virginia.

James M. Buchanan
Charlottesville, Virginia
December, 1957

Public Principles of Public Debt

1. The Economists
and Vulgar Opinion

"Many a citizen will never be able to understand fully the problem of the public debt, for it is too complicated for the average layman. On these technical matters he will have to accept the word of the experts."[1] This statement by Professor Seymour Harris has two noteworthy implications. It is, first of all, a rather severe indictment of the ability of economists to fulfill their educational task. Secondly, it suggests that the experts themselves are agreed on the "truth."

On the face of it, the problem of public debt does not seem complicated. Indeed it seems quite simple when compared with the problem of the circular flow of goods and services in a money economy. Yet it is in regard to the latter problem that great insight has been imputed to businessmen and lay leaders in times past. Critical historians of economic thought may legitimately question the depth of genuine understanding about the unemployment problem contained in the Mercantilists' or Protectionists' "fear of goods" or even in the Reverend Malthus' predictions of a general glut. But economists, especially during the last quarter century, appear to accept almost universally that common everyday opinion on the public debt is fundamentally wrong. Any challenge to this relative unanimity stands in danger of being rejected at the outset. Surely, we are inclined to say, the vulgar ideas about the public debt are grounded in almost pure fallacy, fallacy which is so simple and obvious that we expose it in the early chapters of our elementary textbooks. We use the common lay reasoning on public debt as a particularly good example of the fallacy of composition before we lead the sophomore

1. Seymour E. Harris, *The National Debt and the New Economics* (New York, 1947), p. 25. Cited by permission, McGraw-Hill Book Company.

on to the more stimulating endeavors of serious study. Everyday man-on-the-street opinion on this subject continues to remain less sophisticated than that achieved by the first-week sophomore. The first steppingstone toward economic literacy has not been passed until the whole set of fallacies in the commonly accepted ideas on the public debt is thoroughly exposed, understood, and replaced by the "true" relations.

Businessmen and politicians have continued to be skeptical. They have little faith in the economists, and even if such faith were normally present, particularly strong intuitions on this question of public debt might make them reluctant to "accept the word of the experts." Economist experts have not been granted much additional responsibility in fiscal matters, and the vulgar theory of public debt has not been wholly discarded in public discussion. The fallacies must not be quite so obvious as they are sometimes made to appear.

The genuine critic should always examine both sides of the coin. Even at this stage could it possibly be that the economists have been wrong while vulgar or common opinion has been substantially correct? This question, so seldom asked by capable critics, is always worthy of consideration.

The test of truth in public debt theory is the same as anywhere else, the consensus of informed and intellectually honest men. In spite of the dominance of one particular conception, however, truth has not yet reached the point where it is entirely uninteresting. A re-examination of public debt theory suggests to me that economists have been in error in much of their recent work. This book advances an alternative theory or conception as "true." But the current consensus being in opposition, the burden of proof must rest with me rather than with the new orthodoxy. My efforts to supplant the accepted doctrine with a different one must do more than criticize; they must be successful in converting.

To accomplish such a reversal of ideas is the primary, in fact the only, purpose of this short book. I shall try to show that the vulgar conception of the public debt is the only one which is fundamentally correct and valid generally. The theory of the public debt which is now accepted by most economists is, at base, fallacious.

2. The New Orthodoxy

The currently dominant theory of public debt is called here the "new orthodoxy." I have adopted this term because of the virtual unanimity which is to be found among scholars. The word "new" modifies "orthodoxy," and it should not be taken to suggest that the ideas themselves are "new" or modern. Long before the "new economics" came into existence, articulate statements of the currently ruling theory of public debt are to be found. And, even today, there is far from a one-to-one correspondence between the proponents of the "new economics" and those who accept the new orthodoxy of debt theory. This may be quite simply illustrated by stating that Professor Pigou himself belongs to the latter group.

The new orthodoxy of the public debt is based upon three basic propositions. These are:

1. The creation of public debt does not involve any transfer of the primary real burden to future generations.
2. The analogy between individual or private debt and public debt is fallacious in all essential respects.
3. There is a sharp and important distinction between an internal and an external public debt.

These three propositions are clearly not independent of one another, but this means of classification does provide a useful model for exposition and initial discussion. Each of the three propositions will be discussed in turn; the additional supplementary and qualifying propositions which may legitimately be attributed to the new orthodoxy will be introduced at appropriate points.

This whole chapter might take the form of selected citation from any one or several of the many modern works on public finance or, more particularly, on the public debt. There is some advantage, however, in avoiding the tedium of excessive direct citation at the outset. But in order to convince the still skeptical reader that my purpose is not that of smashing straw men, I shall include one section containing specific references which should prove both necessary and sufficient.

It is especially difficult to present an argument objectively without appearing to support it. In the discussion which follows I shall assume the position of an advocate of the new orthodoxy and present the argument as I think he would. This procedure will provide for efficiency and clarity, and it will eliminate continual repetition of qualifying phrases such as "the ruling theory holds," "the new orthodoxy alleges," and so forth. This initial warning should be sufficient to prevent any direct citation out of proper context.

"We Cannot Mortgage the Future"

The process of government borrowing transfers current purchasing power from the hands of individuals or institutions to the government. The utilization of this purchasing power by the government employs resources in the same general time period as that in which the borrowing operation takes place. Insofar as these resources are drawn from private employments, the full opportunity cost, that is, the real cost, of the public expenditure is held to be borne by those individuals living in the initial or "current" time period. The real sacrifice of private goods and services, that is, real income, allegedly occurs during this initial period, and this sacrifice stems, not from the debt *per se,* but rather from the decision of the government to undertake the public expenditure in question. In this particular respect, the financing of a public expenditure by borrowing is little different from financing it by taxation. In either case, the "real" burden is borne currently. Any shifting of the primary real burden of public expenditure over time by changing the method of financing is impossible.

The loan method of financing, as opposed to the tax method, does, of course, involve different effects on individuals living in time periods following that of the debt creation. Debt issue leaves "future" generations with a heritage of both claims and obligations. But these claims and obligations can represent no aggregate real burden because they cancel each other, at least for the internally held public debt. Individuals living in "future" generations are obligated to pay sufficient taxes to service the debt, that is, to meet the interest and amortization charges, but these revenues collected in taxes are returned to this same generation in the form of interest payments on debt instruments held by individuals within the same economy. Therefore, the debt places on individuals of "future" generations nothing more than some obligation to make some transfers among themselves. There can be no real sacrifice of resources involved in this transfer. This transfer is not at all comparable with the sacrifice of resources which was borne during the period when the debt was originally created and the public expenditure carried out.

The public debt is, of course, not burdenless. Early advocates of the modern view admittedly overlooked the possibility that the process of making the required interest transfers involves a net burden. However, this brush of excessive enthusiasm was quickly discounted by more sober heads, and general recognition is now given to the fact that the heritage of public debt does create serious problems of transfer. These transfer burdens are essentially of a "frictional" or "stresses and strains" variety. This secondary transfer burden, as distinct from the primary real burden, depends on numerous variables. Significant among these is the distribution of the debt instruments. If the taxpayers are roughly identical to the bondholders, there is no serious transfer burden, but if these two groups are widely different in make-up, real costs are imposed on the "net" taxpayers, and real benefits on the "net" interest receivers. The full recognition of the existence of such a transfer burden does not, however, invalidate the first fundamental principle of the new orthodoxy: The primary real burden cannot be shifted to future generations. The secondary transfer burden is akin to the frictional or incentive burden of collecting taxes currently, if this method were to be chosen in lieu of the public loan. These are second-order real costs or burdens, over and above that represented by the direct or primary sacrifice of resources actually withdrawn from private usage and subsequently employed by government. This primary burden must always rest with the individuals living in the time period during which the government utilizes the resources.

The recognition of this homely fact should presumably remove substantially the suspicion that governments, if allowed too much access to the loan method of financing, might overspend on frivolous public projects. Only those misguided laymen and politicians can now entertain such suspicions, for the analysis clearly reveals that governments do not, in effect, postpone paying the real costs of expenditure when it is directly undertaken. The loan is fundamentally a form of a tax, in many cases the ideal form.

"The False Analogy"

The key to an understanding of the perseverance of the vulgar fallacies is provided in the proclivity of individuals to extend family and institutional standards of accounting to government. Public finance is considered analogous to private finance. This analogy is fundamentally fallacious, especially when problems of internal public debt are considered. Therefore, a central feature of the new orthodoxy is its demonstration of the conceptual distinctions which must be made between the two accounting standards.

To the individual or the private institution, the interest charges which are necessary to service a private debt clearly represent a real burden. Either consumption spending or savings must be reduced, and purchasing power transferred to the holder of the debt claim. The private debt is in this way analogous to the external public debt. But if the public debt is internal, the holders of the claims are from the same group of individuals as the taxpayers. No net real income is transferred outside the budget of the collective entity.

The individual, in creating a debt, is deliberately placing an obligation on his expected real income over future time periods. He is effectively transferring or shifting the burden of payment for whatever expenditure he undertakes to future time periods. He is changing the time shape of his income flow. This being acknowledged, he should exercise caution and restraint in making expenditures which can only be financed by borrowing. It is entirely possible that excessive borrowing can place such a weight on future income that the individual may be threatened with bankruptcy.

Almost none of these conclusions hold with equal force, however, when the internal public debt is considered. Since all resources employed in making the expenditure must come from within the economy initially and must be used up in the initial time period, there can be no shifting of the primary real burden forward in time. The time shape of the community's income stream is not modified substantially. Therefore, the ordinary prudence suggested for the private individual is not fully applicable as advice to the national government, although subordinate governmental units are acknowledged to be similar here in all relevant respects to the private individual. The frictional or transfer burden placed on future incomes of the community through the necessity of making interest transfers is a real one, but it is surely minor relative to the primary burden which is fully shifted forward in the individual debt. There is little or no danger that the government could go bankrupt regardless of the size of its internal debt.

All of this suggests that "living beyond its income" is not an overriding consideration for the national government. The excess of expenditure over revenues is nothing to cause especial concern, and this condition may be necessary and beneficial during certain phases of the business cycle. The rule of budget balance which properly dictates the behavior of the private family may represent an especially dangerous myth when it is applied to national governments. Deficit financing and, by implication, debt creation, may be a permanent and necessary feature of the modern public economy.

The size of the public debt is of relatively little concern for the public economy because the debt carries with it claims as well as obligations. To individuals who own the bonds, public debt is an asset. And since these individual bondholders live in the community along with the taxpayers, the value of the asset just matches the value of the liability represented by the debt at any chosen point in time. For the private individual, his debt is entered as a liability only. The asset side of the debt is held by a "foreigner" insofar as the individual's private budgetary calculus is concerned.

Internal and External Debt

The discussion of the two preceding sections is applicable only to the internal public debt, or so says the new orthodoxy. The impossibility of transferring or shifting the primary real burden forward in time as well as the fallacy in the analogy with private debt stems from the interdependence of the social economy. The public economy, the government, has within its accounting limits both the debtors and the creditors. The debt in such circumstances is a mere financial transaction. No outside resources are imported and employed when debt is created; no net reduction in income flow takes place (aside from the frictional effects of transfer) when interest is paid or the debt is amortized.

If the debt is externally held, however, the analysis must be sharply modified. For external or foreign debt the "classical" or vulgar ideas are almost fully applicable. The primary real burden can effectively be shifted forward in time since there need be no net domestic sacrifice of resources during the period of debt creation. The payment of interest does represent a real burden here because the domestic income stream is reduced by the necessity of transferring resources abroad. Future generations will find their incomes reduced by such transfers. And finally when debt is to be repaid, domestic resources must be transferred to foreigners; this real burden of repayment is also borne by future generations. The analogy with private debt fully holds. External public debt may be a signal of fiscal irresponsibility, something which must be avoided when possible. The rule of budget balance should be replaced by one which reads: Taxes plus internal debt should equal public expenditures.

Line and Verse

I believe that the preceding argument accurately and honestly represents the "new orthodoxy." I can only rely for this on some sort of subjective test which indicates that the argument presents the fundamentals of public debt theory in substantially the way I should have written a textbook chapter on it a few years ago. For purposes of completeness, however, some reference to the literature is indicated, although economists at all familiar with the subject matter field are encouraged to proceed immediately to the next chapter.

Professor Abba P. Lerner occupies a unique, and noteworthy, position in the tradition of the new orthodoxy. In his work, the tradition reaches its extreme logical conclusion, and his contribution in pushing the argument to this point merits high praise. It is sometimes more valuable to complete with full rigor an argument which is at base fallacious than it is to accept the argument generally but to qualify analysis with "yes, but." And there are many "yes, but" statements in the public debt literature of the last quarter century.

Lerner's work on the public debt is best represented in his paper "The Burden of the National Debt," an essay contributed in honor of Alvin H. Hansen.[1] This essay may be characterized as the "standard" model for the new orthodoxy. The following excerpts will suffice:

---

1. Abba P. Lerner, "The Burden of the National Debt," in Lloyd A. Metzler et al., *Income, Employment and Public Policy* (New York, 1948), pp. 255–75. Cited by permission, W. W. Norton and Company.

By far the most common concern about the national debt comes from considering it as exactly the same kind of thing as a private debt which one individual owes to others. . . . (p. 255)

The simple transferability of this rule to national debt is denied by nearly all economists. . . . (p. 255)

One of the most effective ways of clearing up this most serious of all semantic confusions is to point out that private debt differs from national debt in being *external*. It is owed by one person to *others*. That is what makes it burdensome. Because it is *interpersonal* the proper analogy is not to national debt but to *international* debt. . . . But this does not hold for national debt which is owed by the nation to citizens of the *same* nation. There is no external creditor. "We owe it to ourselves." (p. 256)

A variant of the false analogy is the declaration that national debt puts an unfair burden on our children, who are thereby made to pay for our extravagances. Very few economists need to be reminded that if our children or grandchildren repay some of the national debt these payments will be made *to* our children and grandchildren and to nobody else. (p. 256)

Similar statements are to be found in almost any standard modern work on public finance or fiscal policy. "The parallelism of private and public finance is false"; "the analogy just does not hold," says Professor Harris, whom we have previously cited.[2] Professor Hansen says: "A public debt, internally held, is not like a private debt. It has none of the essential earmarks of a private debt."[3] In Professor Harold Groves' widely used textbook we find:

It is easy to demonstrate that, as far as the physical or "objective" burden is concerned, all (or nearly all) must come from the generation that fights the war. . . . To put the argument another way, when a nation borrows from itself or within the family, it may have to tax future generations to pay principal and interest on the debt, but the future generations in turn receive this interest and principal and may, if they like, enlarge their consumption with it.[4]

2. Seymour E. Harris, *The National Debt and the New Economics* (New York, 1947), pp. 25, 55.

3. Alvin H. Hansen, *Fiscal Policy and Business Cycles* (New York, 1941), p. 185.

4. Harold M. Groves, *Financing Government* (New York, 1954), p. 560. Cited by permission, Henry Holt and Company.

We find Pigou stating:

> It is sometimes thought that whether and how far an enterprise ought to be financed out of loans depends on whether and how far future generations will benefit from it. This conception rests on the idea that the cost of anything paid for out of loans falls on future generations. . . . Though twenty-five years ago this idea could claim some respectable support, it is now everywhere acknowledged to be fallacious.[5]

The list of such statements could be extended almost indefinitely, but perhaps one additional citation from what is one of the best current textbooks will be sufficient. Brownlee and Allen, while recognizing the similarities between government and private borrowing, conclude:

> Internally held debts, however, need not impose such burdens on the nation as a whole. There may be losses in that more productive uses for the resources could have been found, . . . but interest payments are made to economic units within the country. The problems associated with internally held debts are frequently problems associated with taxation for any purpose.[6]

The Burden of Transfer

The rediscovery of the transfer payment approach to the public debt and its affinity to the fiscal policy held to be desirable caused its early modern advocates to be somewhat extravagant in their claims. In the years between the appearance of the *General Theory* and World War II, many writers held the public debt to be completely burdenless.[7] This natural overenthusiasm generated a reaction which might have been expected. In the works of Wright, Ratchford, and Meade a more balanced version of the new orthodoxy was

5. A. C. Pigou, *A Study in Public Finance* (3d ed.; London, 1949), p. 38. Citations by permission, Macmillan and Co., Ltd.

6. O. H. Brownlee and E. D. Allen, *Economics of Public Finance* (2d ed.; New York, 1953), p. 127. Cited by permission, Prentice-Hall, Inc.

7. Perhaps the best example is Jorgen Pedersen, whose paper in *Weltwirtschaftliches Archiv* (May, 1937) is cited by Hansen, who is in almost complete agreement with Pedersen. See Hansen, op. cit., p. 142.

achieved.[8] The contribution which these works made lay in their emphasis upon the existence of a real burden of making the internal transfer of resources required in the servicing or the amortization of the domestic public debt. These writers did not dispute the orthodox view that the primary real burden rests on the generation living at the time of debt creation; their emphasis was almost wholly placed on the secondary burden of making the necessary transfers of real income among individuals within "future" generations. These writers were essentially modifiers of the new orthodoxy, not critics. The approach is best summarized in the statement by Wright:

> The layman is likely to consider merely what he would do, if he were confronted by an ever-increasing debt—and is inclined to transfer this picture without modification to the case of national debt. Such a mode of thought is clearly inadequate, but it is equally unwarranted to go to the opposite extreme and deny that an internally held debt can *ever* be a burden. . . .
>
> We may therefore conclude that the statement that an internally held public debt imposes no economic burden on society is not *entirely* true. The burden has been *enormously* exaggerated, but it would be foolish to deny that it does exist.[9] (Italics supplied.)

In still another place, Wright says: "I have tried, in several places, to show the existence of *some* burden."[10] The emphasis is clear; the more extreme versions of the new orthodoxy are not *entirely* correct, and the old view *enormously* exaggerated the burden. All that was presumed to be required was a slight repair job which will allow adequate recognition to be given to the frictional and incentive-induced burdens involved in making the required internal transfers. Quite clearly the taxation which must be levied to service a

---

8. David McCord Wright, "The Economic Limit and Economic Burden of an Internally Held National Debt," *Quarterly Journal of Economics,* LV (November, 1940), 116–29; "Moulton's 'The New Philosophy of the Public Debt,' " *American Economic Review,* XXXIII (September, 1943), 573–90; B. U. Ratchford, "The Burden of a Domestic Debt," *American Economic Review,* XXXII (September, 1942), 451–67; J. E. Meade, "Mr. Lerner on 'The Economics of Control,' " *Economic Journal,* LV (April, 1945), 47–70.

9. Wright, "The Economic Limit and Economic Burden of an Internally Held National Debt," op. cit., 117 and 129.

10. David McCord Wright, "Mr. Ratchford on the Burden of a Domestic Debt: Comment," *American Economic Review,* XXXIII (March, 1943), 115.

large internal debt will exert some effect on incentives to work and to invest in new capital formation. Insofar as these effects are negative, that is, act to reduce real incomes, the transfer payment imposes some burden. But this suggests that proper and careful taxing policy might do much to remove this secondary burden. As Wright suggests: "Careful tax policy could reduce it almost to the vanishing point."[11]

Ratchford explicitly denies that modification in the tax structure could eliminate the secondary burden, and he is somewhat more insistent than Wright on the necessary existence of some real burden of transfer. While Ratchford centers his attention on the retardation of investment, Meade emphasizes the effects of the transfer upon the incentives to work, and he concludes that individuals must work less with a large internal debt than they would without such a debt.

The essential contributions of these economists to debt theory was considered to be *corrective*, not *adverse*, to the main stream of the new orthodoxy. The three bulwarks summarized in the form of the three propositions at the beginning of this chapter were not breached. The influence of these writers in toning down the new orthodoxy has been important, and some recognition of "frictions," "stresses and strains," is to be found in most of the more recent discussions of the subject. But nothing has yet been done toward attacking the central core of the new orthodoxy itself.

New Orthodoxy—Old Ideas

As stated at the beginning of this chapter, it is necessary to emphasize that it is the orthodoxy which is new rather than the ideas which are contained. In this, as in many other respects, the "new" economics has suffered from a failure of its advocates to conduct a careful examination of the existing literature. This seems to have been especially true of the American contributors to the discussion.[12] It may be suggested that if some of the more enthusiastic modern propounders of the newly rediscovered doctrine should have real-

11. David McCord Wright, *The Creation of Purchasing Power* (Cambridge, Mass., 1942), p. 148.
12. Cf. Giannino Parravicini, "Debito pubblico, reddito, occupazione," *Rivista di diritto finanziario e scienza delle finanze* (1951).

ized that the same arguments have been floating around since the early years of the eighteenth century, they might have been encouraged to examine the doctrine somewhat more carefully. The "classical" scholars in public finance were not ignorant of the "transfer" or "false analogy" approach. They knew it, studied it, and, after careful consideration, rejected it.

A conception of public debts strikingly similar to those which are currently orthodox was widely prevalent in the eighteenth century and before, and this was considered an essential part of the whole mercantilist doctrine. Public debts augment the riches of the country, according to the Dutch writer Pinto. And Berkeley called public debts a mine of gold.[13]

One of the first explicit statements of the false analogy argument appears to have been that of J. F. Melon, whose work appeared in 1734. He said: "Les dettes d'un Etat sont des dettes de la main droite à la main gauche, dont le corps ne se trouvera point affaibli."[14] Voltaire stated that the government could not impoverish itself by debt issue. Condorcet argued that public debts were bad only insofar as interest was paid to foreigners.[15] An anonymous writer of *An Essay on Public Credit* (1748) said: ". . . if 60 millions of our debt be the property of the people of Great Britain we are not the richer nor the poorer for that part of the debt."[16] Sir James Stuart clearly accepted the falsity of the analogy between public and private debt.[17] These views were so widely held that Leroy-Beaulieu could say with authority: "Such were the current ideas in the 18th century."[18]

The central features of the doctrine seem to appear in that least likely of all places, Ricardo. He states clearly and precisely that the full primary burden is placed on the current generation and is caused by the government's usage of resources. The interest payments are mere transfers.

13. Paul Leroy-Beaulieu, *Traité de la Science des Finances* (7th ed.; Paris, 1906), Vol. II, p. 223.

14. J. F. Melon, "Essai Politique," Chapter 23 in *Economistes Financiers du 18me siecle*, p. 479. Cited in C. F. Bastable, *Public Finance* (2d ed.; London, 1895), p. 613.

15. Leroy-Beaulieu, op. cit., p. 224.

16. Cited in E. L. Hargreaves, *The National Debt* (London, 1930), p. 74, where, in turn, the citation is taken from a reference in Malachy Postlethwayt, *Dictionary of Trade*.

17. Sir James Stuart, *An Inquiry into the Principles of Political Economy* (1767), p. 625 as cited in Hargreaves, loc. cit., p. 81.

18. Leroy-Beaulieu, op. cit., p. 224.

> When, for the expenses of a year's war, twenty millions are raised by means of a loan, it is the twenty millions which are withdrawn from the productive capital of the nation. The million per annum which is raised by taxes to pay the interest of this loan is merely transferred from those who pay it to those who receive it. . . . The real expense is the twenty millions, and not the interest which must be paid for it.[19]
>
> The argument of charging posterity with the interest of our debt, or of relieving them from a portion of such interest, is often used by otherwise well informed people, but we confess we can see no weight in it.[20]

As we shall show later, the ideas of Ricardo were based upon a highly simplified model which is not fully reflected in these citations taken out of context.

German writers more or less accepted the "productivity" conception of public debt from the outset. Dietzel emphasized the wisdom of public loans,[21] and Wagner stated that the future burden argument was based on a misunderstanding of the simple process of debt creation.[22]

The currently orthodox argument was fully and explicitly recognized by most writers of the late nineteenth and early twentieth century, some of whom accepted it, while others rejected it. In 1896, Knut Wicksell could say, with full approval, that the impossibility of transferring the primary real burden has been often noted.[23] In the great Italian debate over the Ricardian proposition that loans and taxes exert identical effects on the economy, the essential elements of the currently orthodox argument were incorporated.[24] The Colwyn Committee, in its careful and thoughtful analysis, recognized

---

19. David Ricardo, "Principles of Political Economy and Taxation," *Works and Correspondence*, P. Sraffa, ed. (Cambridge: Royal Economic Society, 1951), Vol. I, pp. 244–45. This and subsequent citations by permission Cambridge University Press.

20. David Ricardo, "Funding System," *Works and Correspondence*, ibid., Vol. IV, p. 187.

21. Gustav Cohn, *System der Finanzwissenschaft* (Stuttgart, 1889), pp. 740–43.

22. Adolf Wagner, *Finanzwissenschaft* (Leipzig, 1877), Vol. I, p. 122.

23. Knut Wicksell, *Finanztheoretische Untersuchungen* (Jena, 1896), p. 131.

24. See Maffeo Pantaleoni, "Imposta e debito in riguardo alla loro pressione," *Giornale degli economisti* (1891), reprinted in *Scritti varii di Economia*, Serie Terza (Rome, 1910); Antonio de Viti de Marco, "La pressione tributaria dell' imposta e del prestito," *Giornale degli economisti* (1893); Benvenuto Griziotti, "La diversa pressione tributaria del prestito e dell' imposta," *Giornale degli economisti* (1917), reprinted in *Studi de scienza delle finanze e diritto finanziario* (Milan, 1956), pp. 193–261.

each of the points made in the modern treatment, but tried to frame these with the necessary qualifications.[25]

The above references are perhaps sufficient to indicate that the ideas central to the new orthodoxy are indeed old ones. They have been fully recognized in nearly all pre-Keynesian fiscal theory discussion, as will be further indicated when we review the pre-Keynesian public debt theories in Chapter 8. How then can the burst of enthusiasm for these old ideas be explained? In retrospect, such an explanation seems difficult to construct. But the 1930's were perilous times, and the Great Depression left deep scars. The revolution in economic thought stirred men's souls; the banner of full employment was to be advanced at all costs and against whatever odds. This became the vital center of attention. Little time was available for careful examination of the intellectual stumbling blocks which the old-fashioned ideas on public debt seemed to represent. Out these ideas went, and the "new" ideas were left only to be picked up and carried forward, not by scholars of public debt theory, but by fiscal policy advocates.

25. See *Report of the Committee on National Debt and Taxation* (London, 1927), especially p. 27.

3. The Methodology
of Debt Theory

Before any meaningful analysis of the public debt can take place, it is necessary to examine the methodology within which analysis may properly be conducted. Put more directly, and more correctly, this means that we must know precisely what the problem is before we start trying to reach conclusions concerning its solution. We must be clear as to what we are talking about.

First of all, some classification is required. "Public debt" is far too generic a term to be subjected to incisive analysis without prior classification and specification. A government may borrow for many reasons; the operation may involve large or small sums; the effect can be real or monetary. Before any analysis is complete, all possible cases must be catalogued and each case considered separately if essential differences appear.

There are listed below the specific types of public debt, by characteristic, which shall be discussed. It is noted that the separate types are not mutually exclusive.

1. Public debt issued during periods of substantially full employment of economic resources for the purpose of providing government with funds with which to secure command over real resources.
2. Public debt issued during periods of less than full employment.
3. Public debt issued during periods of threatening inflation and designed only to neutralize monetary resources.
4. "Marginal" issues of public debt which are small enough relative to the whole economy and to the financial market to allow the influences of debt issue upon the interest rate, the absolute price level, and the structure of relative prices to be neglected.

5. "Supra-marginal" issues of public debt for which effects upon the structure of interest rates and prices cannot be neglected, and which must, therefore, be included as a part of the analysis.
6. Public debt issued during war periods and purchased largely by the banking system.
7. Public debt, the proceeds of which are devoted to collective investment in long-term capital projects, which are calculated to yield social income.
8. Public debt, the proceeds of which are invested in self-liquidating public projects which produce monetary revenues.
9. Public debt, the proceeds of which are used wastefully.

The above listing could be extended, but it suffices to indicate the difficulties likely to arise when all of the separate characteristics are neglected and the "public debt" discussed. The listing includes the major characteristics which must be thoroughly examined.

Once we have specified the characteristics of the debt form which we desire to examine, great care must be taken to make an analytical comparison which is methodologically appropriate and which will produce relevant results. This point is an extremely important one, and it provides a key to an understanding of much of the error which has been pervasive, not only in debt theory, but in fiscal theory generally. A brief digression on this general methodological issue seems warranted at this point.

Analysis must consist largely of comparison. The effects of a given change in a variable are discussed normally in terms such as "before and after," or "with and without." In a system embodying many relationships and many variables, it is often highly useful to allow one variable to change and to trace the effects of this change while *neglecting* the changes on the remaining variables of the system. This is the normal procedure in Marshallian partial-equilibrium economics. One variable is allowed to change, for example, one price, with the closely related variables frozen into the other things equal or *ceteris paribus* pound. In this way, the impact of the changed variable on behavior can be isolated and examined, for example, the effect of the change in the single price on the quantity demanded of the single commodity. All users of this method must recognize that many related variables are modified, indeed must be modified, by the initial change imposed on the variable of impact. But if the system is sufficiently large, the offsetting or compensating variation may be so small that these may be neglected for *any one variable*. This is partial-equilibrium analysis in its standard form, but care must always be taken to insure that nothing more than partial equilibrium conclusions may be obtained from it. Any attempt to extend the conclusions reached from the usage of such a model to the total system or economy is doomed to failure and can only produce fallacious results. This is true because, for the total economy, the offsetting changes which may be neglected or put in *ceteris paribus* are, in the aggregate, as important as is the initially imposed change on the variable of impact or action. The analysis is only one-half complete if these offsetting changes are neglected.[1]

What has all of this to do with the theory of the public debt? The variable which we wish to examine is the size of the debt itself. Debt theory should enable us to obtain some rough predictions concerning the effects of issuing debt, or of changing the magnitude of the outstanding debt. But meaningful analysis, and by this we mean analysis which will produce useful predictive results, cannot proceed on the assumption that we can change the debt without anything else in the system changing at the same time. All other variables in the economic system cannot be held in *ceteris paribus* when debt issue is examined. The partial equilibrium approach falls down here, as it does in all of fiscal theory. It is inapplicable for two reasons.

First of all, the system of relationships with which we must work is small. If the number of relationships and the number of variables is not large, *ceteris paribus* as a methodological tool has no place in analysis and is likely to produce more harm than good.[2] A change cannot be imposed on a dependent variable without offsetting changes being introduced elsewhere in the system. And, what is perhaps more important, dependent and independent variables cannot be arbitrarily classified. Economic relationships of dependence and independence alone can determine the appropriate classification.

---

1. Milton Friedman in his outstanding paper, "The Marshallian Demand Curve," *Journal of Political Economy*, LVII (December, 1949), 463–95, has shown how the partial equilibrium approach can be modified to escape this inherent difficulty. In his other works, notably, "The 'Welfare' Effects of an Income Tax and an Excise Tax," *Journal of Political Economy*, LX (February, 1952), 25–33, he has shown how a neglect of the necessary compensating changes has produced serious analytical errors.

2. For a further and extended discussion of this and related points, see my "*Ceteris Paribus*: Some Notes on Methodology," *Southern Economic Journal* (January, 1958).

The second reason why such models fail to be applicable in fiscal theory is that we are almost always interested in general equilibrium or general welfare conclusions. We do not seek sectoral or partial results, but rather results applicable for the whole governmental unit or for the whole economy.[3]

Fiscal theory must always recognize the fundamental two-sidedness of the government's fiscal account. It is not methodologically permissible to examine, for example, a change in the level of taxes without examining, at the same time, the offsetting or compensating changes on the expenditure side, provided that the quantity of money is held unchanged. Similarly, it is not permissible to examine the change in a single tax without, at the same time, analyzing the compensating change in another tax, in government expenditure, or in the money supply. The major contribution which the Italian scholars have made to fiscal theory lies in their continued emphasis on this point, as opposed to the Anglo-Saxon tradition in which the error has persisted and is, even now, vigorously defended.[4]

The general issue may be restated in the following way. Analysis is meaningful only if *relevant* and *realizable* comparisons are made. It would do the engineer little good to attempt to analyze the movements of one side of the teeter-totter on the assumption that the other side remains unchanged, for the other side must change to allow for any initial movement. The two sides are dependent variables, and they cannot be treated as independent for useful analysis.[5]

But let us return to debt theory in a more specific way. The relevance of the methodological issue can be made clear by the use of practical examples. Borrowing is only one means through which the government secures command over monetary resources, which, except in the case of anti-inflationary debt issue, the government uses to purchase real resources. Borrowing is, therefore, an alternative to taxation. If a given public expenditure is to be

---

3. Cf. Gustavo Del Vecchio, *Introduzione alla finanza* (Padua, Italy, 1954), p. 10.

4. For a recent controversy in which the issues are clearly drawn along these lines, see my "Capitalization of Excise Taxes: Comment," *American Economic Review*, XLVI (December, 1956), 974–77, and the reply by J. A. Stockfisch (977–80). For a more general discussion of the issue, see my "La metodologia della teoria dell' incidenza," *Studi economici* (December, 1955).

5. Professor Frisch has recently made essentially this same point in reference to Hotelling's tax analysis. See *Econometrica*, 24 (July, 1956), 311.

financed, this can only be accomplished in three ways: taxes, loans, and currency inflation. The analysis of the effects of debt issue must, therefore, compare what will happen under the debt with what will happen under the tax or inflation.

It is perhaps better to look at the problem in terms of the whole set of fiscal alternatives. Debt creation is an alternative to increased taxation, currency inflation, or expenditure reduction. When we analyze the effects of debt we must always conduct the analysis in differential terms; that is, we must allow one of the three possible compensating variables to be changed in an offsetting way. This is the only permissible means of actually comparing what will happen with and without the debt. If the debt is not to be issued, either taxes must be increased, currency inflation must take place, or the public expenditure cannot be financed. It is wholly improper to hold the level of taxes, the money supply, and government expenditure in *ceteris paribus,* either explicitly or implicitly, when debt issue is examined.[6]

It will be useful to illustrate the methodological issue discussed here by means of a specific example. We may cite the work of Professor J. E. Meade, one of the "modifiers" of the currently ruling theory.

Consider two communities which are *otherwise identical,* but in the first of which there is no internal national debt, while in the second there is a national debt the interest on which is as great as the rest of the national income put together.

	Communities	
	I	II
Net national income at factor cost	100	100
National debt interest	Nil	100
Taxable income	100	200
Rate of taxation	0	50%
Income after tax	100	100

In Community I, individuals earn 100; the state has nothing to pay out, and there is not taxation. Individuals are left with a tax-free income of 100 *on the assurance that they will lose the enjoyment of the whole of any income*

6. This point is recognized by Cesare Brasca, "Intorno agli effetti economici del debito pubblico," *Rivista internazionale di scienze sociale,* XXV (1954), 423.

which they desist from earning. In Community II, individuals earn 100; they receive 100 in interest. . . . Their taxable incomes are, therefore, 200, of which the State takes 100 in taxation to finance the . . . debt interest. Individuals are left (as in I) with a tax-free income of 100, *but this time on the assurance that they will lose only 50% of any increase which they desist from earning.* Naturally, in the second case they will work less hard, and will strike a balance between work and leisure which is more inclined to leisure than the facts of the economic situation really warrant."[7] (First italics only supplied, others in original.)

Professor Meade appears to have committed the methodological error against which we have warned. By his assumption that the communities are *otherwise identical,* he seems to have overlooked the necessary compensating change in some other variable. If the internal debt had not been undertaken, taxes must have been increased, public expenditure reduced, or currency inflation allowed to take place. In the general case some effects upon the incentives to work and to invest would be present under each of these alternatives. And, in this way, the level of real incomes over future time periods would have been modified. In any specific time period, aggregate real income could be less than, greater than, or equal to, that which is present when the debt alternative is examined. There is no *a priori* way to state which of these possibilities is the more likely to occur. Meade's assumption of equivalent real income is, therefore, only one possible case out of many.

Let us place ourselves, for the moment, in the position of an advocate of the extreme "new orthodoxy" in replying to the Meade argument. It could be postulated that, as an alternative to debt creation, public expenditure is reduced, and with it, the level of real income and employment. The amount of resources devoted to capital formation is reduced, and future income streams are correspondingly lowered. With the internal debt, the admitted effects on incentives to work and to invest generated by the necessity of making interest transfers may lower real incomes also. But there is no assurance that the level of real income would be higher without the internal debt than it would be with the debt.

Such a critique of the Meade argument would be quite appropriate since

---

7. J. E. Meade, "Mr. Lerner on 'The Economics of Control,'" *Economic Journal,* LV (April, 1945), 62.

Meade failed to specify carefully the nature of the compensating variation assumed in his analysis. The critic would likely go on to state that, under the conditions outlined in the above paragraph, there is no real burden of public debt when properly considered in a meaningful, differential sense. In this extension of his argument the critic would, however, be committing a *second*, and related, methodological error which has led to much confusion in debt theory. He would be attributing to debt issue the effects of the combined debt-expenditure operation. Although it is essential for sound analysis to consider both sides of a prospective fiscal operation, the effects of changes in the primary variable (debt) must be kept quite distinct from the effects of changes in the compensating variable (in this case, public expenditure).

The two sides of the combined fiscal operation must be kept conceptually distinct. If they become too closely connected, the availability of other, and possibly preferred, alternatives to either half will tend to be overlooked. For example, if the effects of public expenditure which is debt financed are attributed to debt creation, it is likely to be forgotten that the same results could possibly have been achieved by either tax financing or currency creation.

Meade was quite justified in his attempt to eliminate this sort of confusion through his *otherwise equal* assumption. His fault lay in the failure to state explicitly the conditions under which his assumption would prove valid. If he had postulated, as a condition for analysis, that the alternative to debt issue is currency creation and that the period in which the choice among these two relevant alternatives is made is characterized by Keynesian-type unemployment, there would be no differential income effects other than those directly attributable to debt issue *per se.* The differential effects between the two relevant alternatives would, in this case, reduce to those of debt issue only. This sort of model is, however, extremely limited in its applicability. In the more general case, each side of the fiscal operation will have separable effects which must be analyzed separately. If debt issue is employed as a means of financing expenditure, fiscal analysis must attempt to isolate the effects of debt issue from those of the expenditure. Or, if debt issue is employed to substitute for taxation, the effects of tax reduction must be separated from those of debt increase. Only in a special sort of model does currency inflation possess no characteristics of taxation. Public debt issue is a means of financing public expenditure, tax reduction, or deflation. Analysis is partial and incomplete which neglects the second half of the transaction; and analysis is apt to misplace emphasis if it fails to keep the two sides conceptually distinct.

As stated earlier, many of the errors in the new orthodoxy may be traced to an oversight of these methodological principles. As a result, conclusions which are true in a broad or general sense become false when applied specifically. This will become evident in the more-extended discussion of both war debt and depression debt in later chapters, but an illustration will be useful at this point. The burden of a war must fall largely upon the generation living during the war period. This conclusion is supported by the argument of this book and by the new orthodoxy. But the conclusion is true only to the extent that taxation or inflation occurs. It is improper to attribute this burden to debt issue rather than to the inflationary spending which debt issue makes possible, for in so doing, the relevant alternative, which is direct currency creation, tends to be overlooked. Debt issue is a means of raising funds, not of spending them, and a meaningful general theory of public debt must recognize this point.

4. Concerning Future Generations

The new orthodoxy of the public debt is based upon three propositions. If these propositions can be shown to be false, the modern conception of public debt must be radically revised. If these propositions can be shown to be true in reverse, the conception must be completely discarded. I shall attempt, in this and the following chapters, to accomplish this reversal. I shall try to prove that, in the most general case:

1. The primary real burden of a public debt is shifted to future generations.
2. The analogy between public debt and private debt is fundamentally correct.
3. The external debt and the internal debt are fundamentally equivalent.

The Analytical Framework

Initially I shall discuss public debt in what may be called its "classical" form. The existence of substantially full employment of resources is assumed. Secondly, I shall assume that the debt is to be created for real purposes, not to prevent or to promote inflation. The government desires to secure command over a larger share of economic resources in order to put such resources to use. This assumption suggests that debt instruments are purchased through a transfer of existing monetary units to the government. Thirdly, I shall assume that the public expenditure in question is of a reasonably limited size relative to both the total income and investment of the community, and, consequently, that the effects of the sale of government securities on the interest rate and the price structure are negligible. Fourthly, I shall assume that the funds used to purchase government securities are drawn wholly from private capital formation. I shall also assume that competitive conditions prevail throughout the economy. Finally, I shall make no specific assumption concerning the purpose of the expenditure financed. I shall show that this purpose is not relevant to the problem at this stage of the analysis.

These assumptions may appear at first glance to be unduly severe. They will, of course, be relaxed at later stages in the argument, but it is perhaps worthwhile to point out that these assumptions are largely applicable to the debt problem as it has been, and is being, faced in the 1950's. They apply, by and large, to the highway financing proposals advanced by the Clay Committee in early 1955. They apply, even more fully, to the debt problems facing state and local units of government, which alone borrowed more than five and one-half billions of dollars in 1956.

By contrast, the assumptions do not accurately reflect the conditions under which the greater part of currently outstanding public debt has been created. This qualification may appear to reduce somewhat the generality of the conclusions reached. Such is, however, not the case. The initial restriction of the analysis to public debt in the "classical" form allows the characteristic features of real debt to be examined; other forms of public debt are less "pure," and it is appropriate that they be introduced only at a second stage of analysis. When this is done in later chapters, the conclusions reached from the initial analysis will be found generally applicable, and the apparently contradictory conclusions stemming from the new orthodoxy will be explained on the basis of the methodological confusion discussed in Chapter 3.

The first of the three basic propositions will now be examined in the light of the specific assumptions stated above.

The Shifting of the Burden to Future Generations

Before we can proceed to discuss the question of the possible shifting of the debt burden, we must first define "future generations." I shall define a "future generation" as any set of individuals living in any time period following that in which the debt is created. The actual length of the time periods may be arbitrarily designated, and the analysis may be conducted in terms of weeks, months, years, decades, or centuries. The length of the period *per se* is not relevant. If we choose an ordinary accounting period of one year and if we further call the year in which the borrowing operation takes place, t_0, then individuals living in any one of the years, $t_1, t_2, t_3, \ldots t_n$, are defined as living in future "generations." An individual living in the year, t_0, will normally be living in the year, t_1, but he is a different individual in the two time periods, and, for our purposes, he may be considered as such. In other words, I shall not be concerned as to whether a public debt burden is transferred to our children or grandchildren as such. I shall be concerned with whether or not the debt burden can be postponed. The real question involves the possible shiftability or nonshiftability of the debt burden in time, not among "future generations" in the literal sense. Since, however, the "future generation" terminology has been used widely in the various discussions of the subject, I shall continue to employ it, although the particular definition here given should be kept in mind.

What, specifically, do the advocates of the new approach mean when they suggest that none of the primary real burden of the public debt can be shifted to future generations? Perhaps the best clue is provided in a statement from Brownlee and Allen: "The public project is *paid for* while it is being constructed in the sense that other alternative uses for these resources must be sacrificed during this period."[1] (Italics mine.) The resources which are to be employed by the government must be withdrawn from private employments during the period, t_0, not during any subsequent period.

This last statement is obviously true, but the error lies in a misunderstanding of precisely what is implied. The mere shifting of resources from private to public employment does not carry with it any implication of sacrifice or payment. If the shift takes place through the voluntary actions of private people, it is meaningless to speak of any sacrifice having taken place. An elemental recognition of the mutuality of advantage from trade is sufficient to show this. If an individual freely chooses to purchase a government bond, he is, presumably, moving to a preferred position on his utility surface by so doing. He has improved, not worsened, his lot by the transaction. This must be true for each bond purchaser, the only individual who actually gives up a current command over economic resources. Other individuals in the economy are presumably unaffected, leaving aside for the moment the effects of the public spending. Therefore, it is impossible to add up a series of zeroes and/or positive values and arrive at a negative total. The economy,

---

1. O. H. Brownlee and E. D. Allen, *Economics of Public Finance* (2d ed.; New York, 1954), p. 126. Also, see Henry C. Murphy, *The National Debt in War and Transition* (New York, 1950), p. 60.

considered as the sum of the individual economic units within it, undergoes no *sacrifice* or *burden* when debt is created.

This simple point has surely been obvious to everyone. If so, in what sense has the idea of burden been normally employed? The answer might run as follows: To be sure no single individual undergoes any sacrifice of utility in the public borrowing process because he subscribes to a voluntary loan. But in terms of the whole economy, that is, in a macro-economic model, the resources are withdrawn from private employment in the period of debt creation, not at some subsequent time. Therefore, if this sort of model is to be used, the economy must be treated as a unit, and we may speak of a *sacrifice* of resources during the initial time period. In the macro-economic model we are not concerned with individual utilities, but with macro-economic variables.

It is perhaps not surprising to find this essentially organic conception of the economy or the state incorporated in the debt theory of Adolf Wagner,[2] but it is rather strange that it could have found its way so readily into the fiscal theory of those countries presumably embodying democratic governmental institutions and whose social philosophy lies in the individualistic and utilitarian tradition. The explanation arises, of course, out of the almost complete absence of political sophistication on the part of those scholars who have been concerned with fiscal problems. With rare exceptions, no attention at all has been given to the political structure and to the possibility of inconsistency between the policy implications of fiscal analysis and the political forms existent. Thus we find that, in explicit works of political theory, English-language scholars have consistently eschewed the image of the monolithic and organic state. At the same time, however, scholars working in fiscal analysis have developed constructions which become meaningful only upon some acceptance of an organic conception of the social group.[3]

In an individualistic society which governs itself through the use of democratic political forms, the idea of the "group" or the "whole" as a sentient being is contrary to the fundamental principle of social organization. The individual or the family is, and must be, the basic philosophical entity in this

2. Adolf Wagner, *Finanzwissenschaft* (Leipzig, 1877), Vol. I, p. 122.

3. For a further discussion of this point, see my "The Pure Theory of Government Finance: A Suggested Approach," *Journal of Political Economy,* LVII (1949), 496–505.

society. This being true, it is misleading to speak of group sacrifice or burden or payment or benefit unless such aggregates can be broken down into component parts which may be conceptually or actually imputed to the individual or family units in the group. This elemental and necessary step cannot be taken with respect to the primary real burden of the public debt. The fact that economic resources are given up when the public expenditure is made does not, in any way, demonstrate the existence of a *sacrifice* or *burden* on individual members of the social group.

The error which is made in attributing a *sacrifice* to the individual who purchases a security, be it publicly or privately issued, has time-honored status. One of its sources, for there must be several, may lie in the classical doctrine of pain cost. Nassau Senior is generally credited with having popularized, among economists, the notion of abstinence. This concept was introduced in order to provide some philosophical explanation and justification for profits or returns to capital investment. The individual, in abstaining from consuming current income, undergoes the pain of abstinence which is comparable to that suffered by the laborer. Abstinence makes the receipt of profits, in an ethical sense, equally legitimate with wages in the distributive system of the late classical economists.

Traces of this real- or pain-cost doctrine are still with us, notably in certain treatments of international trade theory, but neoclassical economic theory has, by and large, replaced this doctrine with the opportunity cost concept. Here the works of Wicksteed and Knight generally and of Ohlin in particular must be noted. In the neoclassical view, resources command a price not due to any pain suffered by their owners, but because these resources are able to produce alternative goods and services. Resources may be used in more than one line of endeavor. A price, that is, a payment to the resource owner, is necessary in order to secure the resource service. Its magnitude is determined by the marginal productivity of the resource in alternative uses.

This shift of emphasis from the real-cost to the opportunity-cost conception has profound implications, some of which have not yet been fully understood. The real-cost doctrine suggests, for example, that a man is paid because he works, while the opportunity-cost doctrine reverses this and suggests that a man works because he is paid. The emphasis is placed on the individual choice or decision, and the gain or benefit side of individual exchange is incorporated into the theory of market price. The classical economists did not clearly view the distributive share as a price and the distribution of real income as a pricing problem.[4] Neoclassical theory does interpret the distributive share as a price, and the factor market is subjected to standard supply and demand analysis. The mutuality of gain from trade becomes as real in this market as in any other.

It becomes irrelevant whether the individual undergoes "pain" as measured by some arbitrary calculus when he works. If he works voluntarily, he is revealing that his work, when coupled with its reward, enables him to move to a preferred position. The individual is in no sense considered to be *paying for* the output which he cooperates in producing, merely because his productive services enter into its production. I am not, in my capacity as a member of the faculty of the University of Virginia, *paying for* the education of young men merely because my time is spent in classroom instruction, time which I could spend alternatively in other productive pursuits. Clearly the only meaningful *paying for* is done by those parents, donors, and taxpayers, who purchase my services as a teacher. What I am paying for when I teach is the income which I earn and by means of this the real goods and services which I subsequently purchase. Only if a part of my income so earned is devoted to expenditure for education can I be considered to be *paying for* education.

All of this is only too obvious when carefully considered. It is a very elementary discussion of the wheel of income which every sophomore in economics learns, or should learn, on the first day of class. If *sacrifice* or *payment* is to be used to refer both to the producer and the final consumer of goods and services, we are double counting in the grossest of ways; we are *paying* double for each unit of real income. We are denying the existence of the circular flow of real income in an organized market economy.

It is not difficult to see, however, that this error is precisely equivalent to that committed by those who claim that the real payment or sacrifice of resources must be made by those living in the period of public debt creation.

---

4. For the best discussion of all these points, see F. H. Knight, "The Ricardian Theory of Production and Distribution," *Canadian Journal of Economics and Political Science,* 1935. Reprinted in F. H. Knight, *On the History and Method of Economics* (Chicago, 1956), pp. 37–88.

The purchaser of a government security does not *sacrifice* resources *for* the public project; that is, he does not *pay for* the project any more than I pay for the education of young men in Virginia. He *pays for* real income in some future time period; he exchanges current command over resources for future command over resources. No payment or sacrifice is involved in any direct sense. The public project is *purchased,* and *paid for,* by those individuals who will be forced to give up resources *in the future* just as those who give up resources to pay my salary at the University of Virginia pay for education. It is not the bond purchaser who sacrifices any real economic resources anywhere in the process. He makes a presumably favorable exchange by shifting the time shape of his income stream. This is not one bit different from the ordinary individual who presumably makes favorable exchanges by shifting the structure of his real asset pattern within a single unit of time.

All of this may be made quite clear by asking the simple question: Who suffers if the public borrowing is unwise and the public expenditure wasteful? Surely if we can isolate the group who will be worse off in this case we shall have located the bearers of the primary real burden of the debt. But clearly the bondholder as such is not concerned as to the use of his funds once he has received the bond in exchange. He is guaranteed his income in the future, assuming of course that the government will not default on its obligations or impose differentially high taxes upon him through currency inflation. The taxpayer in period t_0 does not sacrifice anything since he has paid no tax for the wasteful project. The burden must rest, therefore, on the taxpayer in future time periods and on no one else. He now must reduce his real income to transfer funds to the bondholder, and he has no productive asset in the form of a public project to offset his genuine *sacrifice.* Thus, the taxpayer in future time periods, that is, the future generation, bears the full primary real burden of the public debt. If the debt is created for productive public expenditure, the benefits to the future taxpayer must, of course, be compared with the burden so that, on balance, he may suffer a net benefit or a net burden. But a normal procedure is to separate the two sides of the account and to oppose a burden against a benefit, and this future taxpayer is the only one to whom such a burden may be attributed.

Widespread intellectual errors are hard to trace to their source. We have indicated that the pain-cost doctrine may have been responsible for some of the confusion which has surrounded public debt theory. But there are other possible, and perhaps more likely, sources for the future burden error. One of the most important of these is the careless use of national income accounting which has grown up in the new economics. Attention is focused on the national or community balance sheet rather than on individual or family balance sheets. In relation to debt theory, this creates confusion when future time periods are taken into account. There is no net change in the aggregative totals which make up the national balance sheet because the group includes both bondholders and taxpayers. The debits match the credits, so no net burden in the primary sense is possible. "Future generations" cannot be forced to *pay for* the resources which have already been used in past periods.

This simple sort of reasoning makes two errors. First, the effect on the national balance sheet is operationally irrelevant. As pointed out above, the nation or community is not a sentient being, and decisions are not made in any superindividual or organic way. Individuals and families are the entities whose balance sheets must be examined if the effects on social decisions are to be determined. The presumed canceling out on the national balance sheet is important if, *and only if,* this is accompanied by a canceling out among the individual and family balance sheets.

A moment's consideration will suggest that genuine canceling in the latter sense does not take place. The balance sheet of the bondholder will include an estimated present value for the bond, a value which is calculated on the certain expectation that the interest payments will be made and the bond amortized when due. These interest payments represent the "future" income which the bondholder or his forbears *paid for* by the *sacrifice* of resources in the initial period of debt creation. These payments are the *quo* part of his *quid pro quo*. They are presumably met out of tax revenues, and taxpayers give up command over the use of resources. This sacrifice of income has no direct *quid pro quo* implication; it is a sacrifice imposed compulsorily on the taxpayer by the decision makers living at some time in the past. To be sure, as pointed out above, if the public expenditure is "productive" and is rationally made, the taxpayer may be better off with the debt than without it. His share of the differential real income generated by the public project may exceed his share of the tax. But the productivity or unproductivity of the project is unimportant in itself. In either case, the taxpayer is the one who *pays,* who *sacrifices* real resources. He is the final "purchaser" of the public goods and services whether he is a party to the decision or not. His is the only sacrifice which is offset, if at all, by the income yielded by the public investment of resources made possible by the debt.

From this analysis it is easy to see that much of the recent discussion on the burden of transfer misses the point entirely. One senses as he reads the discussion, notably that of Ratchford, that underlying the argument for the existence of a transfer burden there is an implicit recognition that the primary real burden does fall on taxpayers of future generations.[5] But the transfer burden advocates were unable to escape the real sirens of the new orthodoxy, the national balance sheet and the false analogy. Their deep and correct conviction that all was not happy in the conceptual underpinnings of the newly rediscovered edifice properly led them to re-examine the theory; but they accepted entirely too much before they started. They gave away their case, and their efforts resulted in little more than a slight modification of the theory. They did little more than to force a new emphasis on the secondary burden of making transfers.

The transfer burden analysis suffers the same methodological shortcomings as the more general approach of the new orthodoxy. If public debt issue is analyzed in terms of the whole set of relevant alternatives, in this case notably that of taxation, the burden associated with the making of an interest transfer cannot fail to be viewed as a primary one akin to that which is imposed through taxation. The failure to consider the position of the individual bondholder under each of the alternative situations led the "transfer burden" analysts to accept the fundamental premise of the new orthodoxy, that interest payments do, in a differential sense, represent a net "transfer" among individuals within the economy.

The Ricardian Approach

We may now discuss the unique set of assumptions under which the primary real burden of the debt cannot be shifted forward in time. And surprisingly enough, this is not mentioned in the new orthodoxy at all. It is propounded

---

5. B. U. Ratchford, "The Burden of Domestic Debt," *American Economic Review,* xxxii (September, 1942), Pt. IV. Abbott, in his work on debt management, appears also to recognize implicitly that the primary real burden of debt is borne by taxpayers of "future generations." He does not, however, discuss this aspect of the problem directly. See Charles C. Abbott, *Management of the Federal Debt* (New York, 1946).

by the classical economist, David Ricardo. Ricardo enunciated the proposition that the public loan and the extraordinary tax exert equivalent effects on the economy. His argument is as follows:

> When, for the expenses of a year's war, twenty millions are raised by means of a loan, it is the twenty millions which are withdrawn from the productive capital of the nation. . . . Government might at once have required the twenty millions in the shape of taxes; in which case it would not have been necessary to raise annual taxes to the amount of a million. This, however, would not have changed the nature of the transaction. An individual instead of being called upon to pay 100£ per annum, might have been obliged to pay 2000£ once and for all.[6]

Under these Ricardian assumptions, the full burden of payment for the public project, whether it be a war or a royal ball, will be borne by the generation which lives at the time of the expenditure. But this is true only because Ricardo assumes that the creation of the debt, with its corresponding obligation to meet the service charges from future tax revenues, causes individuals to write down the present values of their future income streams. The tax reduces the individual's current assets directly; both the gross and net income streams over future time periods are reduced, these being equivalent in this case. The loan does not affect the gross income stream, but it does impose a differential between this and the net income stream. Capitalized values will be figured on the basis of income streams net of tax. Therefore, present values of assets will be immediately reduced by the present value of the tax obligations created by the future service charges. Present values will be identical in the two cases.

This Ricardian reasoning is correct within the framework of his assumptions. But it should be noted first that this is not at all the reasoning of the new orthodoxy. Ricardo places the primary burden of the public loan on the *taxpayer* not the bond purchaser. The primary burden is placed on the taxpayer because he writes down the value of his capital assets in anticipation of his obligation to pay future taxes to service the debt.

This Ricardian proposition has been much discussed in the Italian works

---

6. David Ricardo, "Principles of Political Economy and Taxation," *Works and Correspondence,* P. Sraffa, ed. (Cambridge: Royal Economic Society, 1951), Vol. I, pp. 244–45.

on fiscal theory. This Italian contribution will be treated in some detail in the Appendix to Chapter 8. It will be sufficient at this point to indicate in general terms the deficiencies in the Ricardian proposition. The major objection which has been raised to the proposition is that individuals do not fully discount future taxes. While full discounting may take place for those individuals who own income-earning assets, this reasoning cannot be extended to individuals who own no assets. For the individual owning capital, it is possible that he will write down the value of his assets and transmit them to his heirs at the reduced value. In this case the burden of the tax required to service the debt can be said to be borne entirely by the individual in the initial period. The necessity of transferring income to bondholders will not reduce the present value of expected utilities for future taxpayers because this would have already been discounted for in the past.

For the individual who owns no capital assets, however, this analysis cannot fully apply. Since slavery is not an acceptable institution in the modern world, individuals are not treated as capital assets and traded in accordance with capitalized values. The individual human being as either a capital asset or a liability disappears at death, and his heirs inherit directly neither his asset characteristics nor his liabilities. For this reason, the individual who owns no capital assets will not fully capitalize the future tax burden involved in the interest charges. He will capitalize them, if at all, only within the limits imposed by his effective planning horizon, that is, only to the degree which he, individually, conceives that he will be a future taxpayer. And, since human life is short, much of the debt burden must remain uncapitalized. Therefore, even granting all of the other Ricardian assumptions, which are extremely restrictive, the burden must rest on "future generations," at least to some degree.

Insofar as other individuals who do own capital assets do not plan to submit these intact to their heirs, that is, insofar as family relationships do not make individuals act as if they will live forever, the Ricardian proposition is further weakened. And when the possibility of individual irrationality in discounting future tax payments is introduced, as Ricardo himself recognized, the location of the debt burden on future taxpayers is even more clear.

It must be concluded, therefore, that this Ricardian analysis, as amended, introduces only a slight modification of the conclusions earlier attained. The primary real burden of a public debt is borne by members of the current generation only insofar as they correctly anticipate their own or their heirs' roles as future taxpayers, and take action to discount future tax payments into reductions of present capital values. Insofar as the time horizons of individuals are not infinite, that is, insofar as future individuals are considered to be separated conceptually from present individuals, there must be some shifting of the primary real burden to future generations.

Conclusions

It has been shown in this chapter that the primary real burden of a public debt does rest largely with future generations, and that the creation of debt does involve the shifting of the burden to individuals living in time periods subsequent to that of debt issue. This conclusion is diametrically opposed to the fundamental principle of the new orthodoxy which states that such a shifting or location of the primary real burden is impossible. We have examined the reasons for the widespread acceptance of the nonshiftability argument. We have isolated at least some of the roots of the fallacy. Among these are the pain-cost doctrine and the use of national rather than individual balance sheets.

The primary real burden of the debt, in the only sense in which this concept can be meaningful, must rest with future generations at least in large part. These are the individuals who suffer the consequences of wasteful government expenditure and who reap the benefits of useful government expenditure. All other parties to the debt transactions are acting in accordance with ordinary economic motivations.

5. The Analogy: True or False?

In this chapter I shall examine the second bulwark of the new orthodoxy, the false analogy between the public debt and private debt. The analytical model will be the same as that employed in the preceding discussion; this model essentially embodies the "classical" assumptions. I shall limit the discussion here to the internal public debt since it is almost universally acknowledged that the public debt–private debt analogy is more appropriate when external public debt is considered. Chapter 6 will be devoted explicitly to the internal debt–external debt comparison.

The Basis of the False Analogy

Again we may initially seek to determine precisely what the advocates of the new orthodoxy mean when the falsity of the analogy is proclaimed. This in itself is a difficult task; clarity is not one of the characteristic features of the literature in this field. As was suggested earlier, the clearest statements are likely to be found in the works of the more extreme proponents of the new approach. Pedersen states:

> The state does not obtain the power of disposal over additional funds, for those funds were already within the realm of its power, and might, in fact, have been obtained through taxation.
>
> Thus an internal loan raised by the state is not really a loan in the ordinary sense, since it possesses none of the *essential* characteristics of such a transaction. . . . An internal loan resembles ordinary borrowing only in a purely formal way, and it is obvious that *every* analogy to private borrowing must be completely false.[1] (Italics supplied.)

1. Jorgen Pedersen, as cited in Alvin H. Hansen, *Fiscal Policy and Business Cycles* (New York, 1941), p. 142.

As a second example we may cite Nevins' more recent work:

> ... internal borrowing by a government in *no* sense represents an addition to the wealth of a society, so interest and capital payments by a government in *no* sense represent a reduction in the disposable wealth of the society. ... A private person may live beyond his income and encroach upon the wealth available to his descendants, but since—apart from the international transfers which are excluded from the present context—a society cannot live beyond its means through the mere creation of monetary debt, such debt cannot constitute a drain on the resources available to future generations.[2] (Italics mine.)

Several points are immediately evident from a first glance at the above statements. The first is that the false analogy argument is not independent of either the future burden argument or the internal-external debt argument, as we have previously noted. Any discussion of one of the three basic propositions must involve some consideration of the other two. Hence, to discuss each of the three propositions separately must introduce considerable redundancy. The second point to be made is that the emphasis is placed on the effects on the national balance sheet. The third point which strikes the reader is the apparent simplicity, and, by inference, the obvious validity of the analysis. This simplicity is important because it serves to mask errors which reasonable scholars would otherwise never have committed.

The Factual Statements

When an internal debt is created, resources for public use are withdrawn from private uses *within* the economy. Therefore, the creation of debt and the correspondent financing of the public project does nothing toward increasing or adding to the wealth of the society. This is, of course, fundamentally correct as a first approximation and requires no difficult reasoning for its comprehension.[3]

---

2. Edward Nevins, *The Problem of the National Debt* (Cardiff, 1954), pp. 22–23. Cited by permission, University of Wales Press.

3. At a slightly more sophisticated level of analysis, however, even this statement must be qualified. In abstract terms, its validity requires that the marginal productivities of the

The Inferences from the Facts

The new orthodoxy draws incorrect inferences from correct factual state-ments. Although it is not made explicit in the statement cited above, the in-ference is clear that the individual (or the public entity which borrows exter-nally) is able, in some way, to increase his wealth by a borrowing operation.[4] The beginning sophomore in accounting can see through the fallacy con-tained in this inference. The asset secured is precisely offset by the liability incurred (the debt). The balance sheet of the borrower is not affected oth-erwise. No change in net worth occurs in the objective sense, if we may as-sume that the borrower does not capitalize favorable expectations immedi-ately. The case is even more clear for the lender. He will write down his one asset item, let us say, cash, which he uses to purchase the private security, to extend the private loan. He will write up another asset item, let us say, loans receivable. No change in net worth takes place. To be sure the borrower se-cures the command over a greater quantity of resources currently, but this does not affect his objectively determined wealth position. The lender, on the other hand, gives up some current command over resources, but this, in it-self, does not reduce his net worth. This command over current resources is replaced with a claim on future resources which carries a present value.

----

resources involved be equal in public and private employments, that the operation be "at the margin." This begs more questions than it answers, however, since the whole issue of evaluating resource productivity is immediately raised. By the nature of public goods, market prices are not available to assist in such comparative evaluation. The shift of re-sources from public to private employments or vice versa can only be adjudged to add to social wealth on the basis of individuals' revealed preferences in supporting the shift. If we assume that a debt creation–public expenditure decision is rationally made, the tax-payer group must be adjudged as having moved to a preferred position. In this sense, therefore, social wealth may be said to have been increased. But the lending as well as the borrowing group must have also benefited, at least in the *ex ante* subjective sense. Gains from exchange are mutual, and some advantages are expected by both parties to the con-tract. Lenders assume that they will receive some differential return from the government security (in terms of rate, lowered risk, or other considerations) while borrowers (taxpay-ers) must be credited with assuming that the public project yields a "social" rate of return in excess of the borrowing rate. The wealth of both groups, which include, of course, many of the same individuals, increases in the subjectively calculated sense. It is evident, however, that this is not the sort of increase denied in the citation quoted in the text.

4. Over and above the gain from making the exchange which is necessary for any mar-ket transaction to be rational. See the preceding footnote.

We may now proceed to examine more carefully the accounting aspects of an internal or domestic public borrowing operation. Let us initially assume that the rate of interest to be paid on government securities is equal to the rate of return on private investments made at the margin. This amounts to assuming that the operation is a marginal one for the bond purchaser. Let us further assume that the public project is of such a nature that individuals do not take its value into account when making up their individual balance sheets. We shall also assume that these same individuals do not capitalize future tax payments. These last two assumptions appear realistic enough for most cases of public borrowing.

When the bond purchaser buys the government bond, he draws down some other asset, let us say cash or private bonds, and replaces this with the government securities. No change in his net worth takes place. By assumption, the taxpayer neither includes the capital value of the public asset nor the discounted value of future tax payments in his balance sheet. Therefore, in the aggregate, individual balance sheets are not affected by the public debt creation. We must conclude, therefore, that, for the period when the public debt is initially created, there is no difference between the internal public debt and private debt. There is no fallacy in the analogy to this point.

When the periods subsequent to this initial one are considered, the analogy would seem to be on more shaky ground. How can the payment of interest on a public debt, in itself, represent a reduction in aggregate individual net wealth since domestic bondholders receive the interest paid as taxes by domestic taxpayers? Yet clearly the payment of interest on a private debt represents a drainage from the real income stream of the individual, a reduction in his net worth.

This comparison must be examined more carefully. How are individual balance sheets affected by the payment of interest on a public debt? We shall continue to make the same assumptions about the nature of the project. The payment of taxes, say out of cash, will reduce the asset side of the taxpayer's account. This will be offset by a reduction in net worth on the right side. The receipt of interest will increase the cash position of the bondholder and, on the right side of his account, net worth will be increased. This increase in net worth of the bondholder just offsets the decrease in net worth of the taxpayer. No change in individual net worth, considered in the aggregate, takes place. The analogy with private debt appears to be false.

There is, however, a subtle fallacy hidden in the above reasoning, and it is based on the methodological error against which we warned in an earlier chapter. The analysis reflects a failure to compare relevant alternatives. This may be most easily shown by examining the implications of the conclusions reached above. According to this analysis, no change in aggregate wealth occurs either when the debt is created or when the interest is paid. From this it should follow that, if the public project yields any positive real income at all, the society achieves a net gain in real wealth as a result of the combined debt issue–public expenditure operation. Any rate of return on the public investment greater than zero would be sufficient to justify public investment. A public policy of ever-expanding public borrowing would seem to be indicated. These implications apparently run counter to those reached in Chapter 4, where it was shown that the "productivity" of the public project must be compared with the costs imposed on "future" taxpayers.

There is something obviously wrong here which must be searched out and corrected. Let us recall the assumptions of our model. Resources are fully employed; in order to utilize resources in public employment, some rate of return in private employment must be sacrificed. Therefore, if the project is completely wasteful, the sacrifice in private wealth is not offset by any gain in "social" wealth. But why does this fail to show up when we consider the individual balance sheet adjustments as we have done above?

The answer lies in the assumption that the net worth of the bondholder is uniquely increased by the receipt of interest on the government security. This reflects an oversight of the fact that capital investment has alternative employments in the private economy, and that some increase in net worth would accrue to individuals who are net creditors in the absence of the public borrowing operation. Differentially speaking, it is not proper to offset the increase in net worth of bondholders which is occasioned by the interest receipts against the decrease in net worth of the taxpayers occasioned by the interest payments. The increase in net worth of the bondholders would have occurred without the public debt; *only the decrease in net worth of the taxpayers may be attributed to the fiscal operation under consideration.* This modification now allows sensible conclusions to be drawn regarding the merits of the debt–public expenditure operation. The differential decrease in net worth imposed upon future taxpayers by the servicing of the debt may be offset against the rate of return on the public project which is debt financed. Quite clearly the project which yields a zero rate of return is not justifiable.

This result is not changed if we modify the assumptions and allow that individuals include both the present capitalized value of the public project and the capitalized value of future tax obligations in their balance sheets. These two are offsetting items, as may readily be demonstrated. Assume now that individuals fully value the public investment project, but that they also recognize the present value of the future tax liability to which they will be subject. The balance sheets of individuals will contain an additional asset item and an additional liability item. Individuals' net worths are not changed by this modification except insofar as these two items differ. But if the present value of future tax payments is fully incorporated into the balance sheet, we cannot then also say that the actual payment of these taxes represents a reduction in individual net worth. The individual will have discounted the necessity for paying taxes; that is, he will have become a Ricardian man. We cannot offset any additional reduction in net worth in periods subsequent to the initial one against the increase in net worth enjoyed by the bondholder who receives interest payments.

The objection may be raised at this point that the bondholder also capitalizes his interest receipts, in fact, that only this process provides a current capital value for the bond. Therefore, it may be objected, if full capitalization of the liability item prevents an interest outpayment from reducing debtor net worth, will not the full capitalization of the asset item prevent the interest receipt from increasing creditor net worth? The answer is no. The debtor-creditor sides of the account here are not symmetrical. The asymmetry stems from the fact that an individual or institution holding a net asset position, that is, who has positive net worth, is in a position to increase his net worth over time. If accounting practice dictates that the individual creditor carry the interest item on an accrual basis, the actual receipt of interest payments will not increase net worth. But net worth between the beginning and the end of the accounting period will have increased by the amount of the interest payment in this case and this will be shown on the asset side of the balance sheet as "accrued interest not yet received." The assumption of full discounting does not modify the conclusion reached. The reduction in net worth of the taxpayer must be offset only against the current value of the public project, not against the current value of the asset held by the lender.

A simple example will serve to demonstrate the whole analysis, although it will perhaps contain some repetition. Let us specifically assume that the public expenditure which is debt financed is completely wasteful, let us say, the funds are used to provide air-conditioning units for the natives of Attu Island. We assume no capitalization of either the future benefits or the future taxes. We have shown that, under these assumptions, no reduction in aggregate individual net worth takes place when the debt is created and the expenditure made. In subsequent periods, the increase in the net worth of the bondholders is just offset by the decrease in the net worth of the taxpayers. Both groups live within the confines of the same economy; therefore the community, taken as a whole, appears to be no richer or poorer by the operation.

The analysis is rescued only when the positions of taxpayers and bondholders are compared in situations with and without the debt, the only comparison which is meaningful and useful for policy purposes. Let us say that the only alternative to debt issue is expenditure contraction; taxation, either directly or through currency inflation, is not possible. If the debt is not contracted, the public expenditure project will not be undertaken. The natives on Attu must do without air conditioners. As a further simplifying assumption, we say that the sacrificed rate of return on private investments is just matched by the return on government securities.

We may now examine carefully the positions of the individual bond purchaser-holder under each of these two possible situations. If the public debt is issued, the individual will transform a private security into a government bond. And while isolated individuals may transform liquid assets such as cash into securities, unless the debt issue generates net dishoarding, the over-all result must be represented by a transformation of private investment funds, actual or potential, into government securities. No change in the net worth of the bond purchaser takes place immediately. When he receives interest on the security, or when interest accrues, his net worth increases. This increase is not greater than the increase in net worth which *would have occurred* had he devoted his funds initially to private rather than public uses. His position is identical in the two situations. Relaxing our simplifying assumptions, his position will be different only insofar as the interest paid on public debt differs from that which he could have earned on private investment after these comparative employments are adjusted for differences in risk premiums. In the differential sense, the bondholders' net worth is not increased by debt issue, *per se.*

The story for the taxpayer is, however, different. As we have shown, he undergoes no reduction or increase in his net worth during the period in which the public loan is floated, except insofar as future tax payments are capitalized and reflected in capital values of assets currently held. (We have assumed in this example that such capitalization does not take place.) When interest is paid in subsequent periods, the net worth of the taxpayer is reduced by the amount of the service charge on the debt. If, on the other hand, the public debt is not issued, and the public expenditure abandoned, the taxpayer presumably undergoes no change in his private net worth at either the time of the possible debt creation *or* in subsequent periods. Thus, we conclude that if the analysis is properly carried out, the public debt does reduce the net worth of the borrower (the taxpayer) during the periods in which interest must be paid, and this reduction is differential in that it takes place *only* if the debt alternative is followed. Of course, for the taxpayer-borrower, this is only one half of the whole fiscal transaction. His final position will depend, in the debt model, upon the productivity of the debt-financed public project relative to the tax-caused reduction in net worth. If the public funds are spent to provide air conditioners for Attu as we have assumed in this example, the taxpayer will find his net worth reduced when interest payments come due, even when both sides of the transaction are fully taken into account, reduced below what such net worth would have been if the original operation had never been undertaken. If, on the other hand, the public funds are used to ward off disaster, that is, to finance a war, the taxpayer will find his net worth increased on balance in spite of the necessity to service the debt. This indicates that the concept of "productivity" must be used broadly and carefully in this context. If the public funds are used to finance a genuine investment project, the real income attributable to that project may more than offset the reduction in net worth generated by the necessity to pay interest. The basic point to be made in all this is simply that the reduction in net worth involved in making the tax payments must be offset against the productivity of the public project which is financed by the debt. It is improper and misleading to offset this reduction in net worth against the increase in net worth enjoyed by the bondholders. The latter increase must take place regardless of the productivity of the public investment.

From this corrected analysis we may conclude that the public borrower (that is, the taxpayer) is at no time in a position different from the private borrower. The analogy between the two holds good in all of the essential respects. If the private borrower uses his borrowed funds foolishly, he will find that his real income is reduced when the necessity to pay interest arises. If he borrows and invests wisely, he may be better off having borrowed although he still must make the interest payments.

The Source of the Error

As we have suggested earlier, the fundamental error made by the new orthodoxy in making a sharp conceptual distinction between public and private debt is methodological. The analysis reflects a failure to consider relevant alternatives. The neglect of the position of the bondholder in the situation without public debt has caused the interest payments to be viewed exclusively as internal transfers. The receipt of interest by bondholders instead of the receipt of real income from the debt-financed expenditure has been viewed as the appropriate offset to tax payments.

This "transfer payment" approach cannot be extended to private debt because the recipient of interest is, by definition, separate from the payer of interest. When discussing private debt the advocates of the new orthodoxy have consistently stressed the "burden" or "sacrifice" involved in both debt servicing and repayment. For example, Lerner speaks of "nearly everybody who has suffered the oppression of private indebtedness."[5] It is, of course, quite proper to attribute a "burden" or "sacrifice" to private debt if care is taken to limit the analysis explicitly to one side of the financial transaction. Debt represents deferred payment, and any payment, considered apart from its return, entails a "burden" on the debtor. Burden in this context can only mean the differential cost or sacrifice imposed by the necessity of making payment when compared with the hypothetical situation in which the same return is secured without obligation. In this way, any outpayment, current or deferred, involves a "burden," and private debt is in no way unique in this respect.

The neglect of the appropriate offset to tax payment, namely, real income from the public project financed, in considerations of public debt led to a similar neglect in considerations of private debt with the result that the latter

5. Abba P. Lerner, "The Burden of the National Debt," in Lloyd A. Metzler et al., *Income, Employment and Public Policy* (New York, 1948), p. 255.

has been viewed as necessarily involving some *net* "burden" or "oppressiveness" even when the full financial transaction is taken into account. This implication is, of course, wholly wrong, and lends support to the usury conception of private finance in which all interest payments are viewed as subsidies to lenders.

The "correct" view of private indebtedness must recognize that the act of borrowing or of lending is a market transaction similar in all its essential respects to other market transactions. Both the borrower and the lender expect, at the moment of contract, to be able to secure advantages from the exchange. The "thing" exchanged in this case is a command over resources at two separate points in time. The borrower secures current command over economic resources, a command which is advanced in time from that which he could otherwise secure without cost. The lender secures a promise of command over resources at some future date. And since resources can be used to produce real income through time, an interest payment or adjustment is necessary to bring the two capital sums into comparable magnitudes. It is commonly stated that interest is a "price" paid for the use of money. This is correct only in a very special sense. The real "price" for the use of money now is the money which must be given up *in the future*. Interest is the differential between these two capital sums converted into a percentage rate.

The perfectly rational individual may choose to borrow for either consumption expenditure or for investment expenditure. In either case, his decision should turn on a comparison of present values. If, when considering a consumption loan, he estimates the utility value of current consumption to exceed the discounted utility value of the payments stream occasioned by the loan, he should borrow. To be sure, once the initial period is completed he will be "oppressed" or "burdened" by the necessity of having to make the payments. But these "burdens" were presumably fully discounted when the loan was considered, and, on balance, the loan transaction involved an expected utility greater than that which would have been forthcoming without the loan. At least this was the calculation at one point in time. The borrower sacrifices some command over resources when he makes the interest payments on his debt. But this is not different in any way from the usual sacrifice involved in any ordinary expenditure. The family sacrifices hamburgers which it could have consumed when it chooses to buy ice cream instead. The fact that this sort of sacrifice occurs simultaneously with the enjoyment of the alternative product serves to obscure the similarity between this and the sacrifice involved in the interest payment on debt. The family who borrows to buy hamburgers today sacrifices hamburgers in the future in order to enjoy them now. The principle is identical for the two cases.

The analysis of private debts is even more clear when we consider private loans made for investment purposes. Here the individual secures command over resources which he puts to directly productive use. Again his decision, if rational, will turn on a comparison of present values, the capitalized value of a future income stream as compared with the capitalized value of a payments stream. If the former exceeds the latter, there is a net gain to be secured from entering the loan market. These two streams need not be equivalent in their time shapes. It is perfectly rational for the individual to borrow on extremely long term to finance short-term projects or vice versa.

Individuals are not, of course, always rational, and their behavior in creating private indebtedness need not reflect wise decision making. But they are likely to be somewhat more rational in their behavior as private individuals than in their behavior as citizens, or at least no less so. The degree of irrationality in the choice process cannot, therefore, lead to a basic distinction between private and public debt.

The implications of the "transfer payment" theory of public debt for the theory of private debt provides us with one explanation of the widespread acceptance of the false analogy argument.[6] There is no essential similarity between public debt, erroneously conceived, and private debt. Nor is private debt, wrongly viewed, similar to public debt properly understood. If private debt is considered necessarily oppressive, burdensome, and all interest payments usurious and unjustified, then the public debt is not comparable. This re-emphasizes that the analogy between the public debt and the private debt, correctly conceived, holds true in most essential respects, at least in the model which we have been considering.

6. There have been few dissents in the literature of the past twenty-five years. One dissent from the prevailing view should, however, be noted. Emerson P. Schmidt argued in 1943 that public debt and private debt are essentially equivalent. ("Private *versus* Public Debt," *American Economic Review,* XXXIII [March, 1943], 119–21.) The fact that his arguments apparently had little effect indicates the dominance of the "new orthodoxy."

Real Balance Effects and the Wealth Illusion[7]

The demonstration of essential similarity does not, however, imply that the two debt forms are identical in all respects. The differences which are present stem largely from the illusion which public debt creation fosters, an illusion rarely present with private debt. As we have said, neither the public asset which is debt financed nor the liability which the debt obligation represents enters normally into individual balance sheet calculations when the debt is created and the asset purchased. This "compensating" illusion does nothing to affect the net worth of the taxpayer-borrower under static conditions. The two debt forms remain equivalent in their influences on individual behavior.

If the absolute price level changes subsequent to debt creation, this public debt illusion may act to exert some differential influence on behavior through the real-balance or Pigou effect. The failure of the public taxpayer-borrower to consider either the asset or the liability side of the transaction may make him immune to such exogenous changes which serve to modify the real value of the one side relative to the other. Although a fall in the absolute price level will tend to increase the real value of the liability relative to the asset, the taxpayer-borrower may not take this into account in his behavior. On the other hand, the fixed-yield claimant, the bondholder, will be affected. He will tend to increase his spending out of income as the real value of his debt claims increases with a decrease in the absolute price level. For the private debt, the borrower will consider explicitly both his debt-financed asset and his liability. A change in the absolute price level will modify the balance-sheet value for each of these, and, if the asset yields income in real terms, its money value will tend to move with the price level. The real value of the liability will move inversely to the price level. Thus, the private borrower will tend to reduce (increase) spending out of income as the price level falls (rises). To some extent, his behavior will offset the real balance reaction of the lender. This offset may be absent for the public debt due to the presence of the illusion.

In discussing this point it becomes necessary to distinguish carefully be-

---

7. I am indebted to Professor A. Morgner for a brief conversation which has caused me to add this section.

tween the illusion fostered at the time of debt creation and that which may be present under the long-continued existence of an outstanding public debt. The taxpayer-borrower may, and probably will, discount both future taxes and future yields on the public asset too heavily when he makes his initial decision. But even if he does this, the subsequent necessity of paying service charges may cause him to take tax obligations more fully into account.

Taxpayers who have grown accustomed to a fixed service charge, say $7 billion annually, will make future plans on the expectation that their tax contribution to this total service charge will remain stable. If the absolute price level is then reduced, this fixed money obligation will assume a greater real value. In this sense, the liability side of the public debt does enter into private behavior similarly to private debt, and the introduction of the real-balance effect does not appear so significant as it might at first have appeared.

The difference caused by the real-balance effect does, however, constitute a difference in the two debt forms, which should not be overlooked. Some critics will dispute perhaps my claim that this difference is not an essential or fundamental one. Be this as it may, the point is that this sort of difference is not that which has been emphasized by the new orthodoxy. The difference discussed here is not due to some fallacy of composition. The difference arises solely out of the greater complexity of the collective choice process which tends to render private shares of both assets and liabilities indistinguishable to the individual participant. The importance of this difference for real-world problems is lessened when a careful distinction between real debt and monetized debt is introduced. As later chapters will demonstrate, much of what we call public debt creation is disguised currency creation. In this circumstance, relevant comparison with private debt is modified. For real-debt issue, the possible differences arising from the real-balance effect merit consideration, but these do not require a reversal of the earlier statement that the two debt forms are fundamentally similar.

Appendix: An Accounting Summary

In the discussion above, individual balance sheets have been frequently used indirectly. It will perhaps be useful to employ them more specifically here and to diagram some of the analysis in terms of simple balance sheet examples.

The simple T-accounts of Table I require little explanation. It is noted that, in the last set of accounts, the lender is in an equivalent position with and without the debt. But the taxpayer-borrower is in a worse position with the debt than he would be without it. He would be better off had the public investment never been undertaken. This result stems, of course, from the assumption that the project financed is completely unproductive. The situation would be identical for a private borrower who has made a wasteful expenditure which he financed by a private loan.

In Table II we assume that the public project is equally productive with private investment. Here it is noted that all parties to the transaction are in identical situations with and without the public debt. In Table III we assume that the public investment is of greater productivity than private investment. Here it is noted that the taxpayer-borrower is in a better position with the public debt than he would have been without it. The position of the lender is not modified. From these three tables it is evident that it is the position of the taxpayer-borrower that is modified by the relative productivity of the public investment.

In Table IV we retain the assumption of Table II that the public and private investments are equally productive, but we now assume that both the value of the project and the future tax payments are fully discounted into present values which are incorporated into individual balance sheets. The results are the same as for Table II. In any future income period, all parties are in identical positions with and without the debt.

In each of the first four tables, it is implicitly assumed that the alternative to public debt is a failure to carry out the proposed expenditure operation. In order to bring the closeness of the analogy with private debt more clearly into the open, Table V assumes that the same individuals who are the taxpayer-borrowers create a whole set of private loans to finance the same project. As may be seen, the position of the borrower is identical in the two situations.

Many other comparisons could be drawn on simple tables such as these, using other assumptions about relative rates of yield, rates of interest on government securities, and the proclivity of individuals to consider public assets and public liabilities as individual assets and liabilities.

It must be emphasized that these simple T-accounts represent only partial balance sheets. In most cases, a bondholder will also be a taxpayer-borrower.

Table I

	With Public Debt				Without Public Debt			
	Lender		**Borrower-Taxpayer**		**Lender**		**Borrower-Taxpayer**	
Period t_0 (before debt is issued)								
	EA—1	L—0, NW—1	EA—1	L—0, NW—1	EA—1	L—0, NW—1	EA—1	L—0, NW—1
Period t_0 (after debt is created)								
	EA—0, GB—1	L—0, NW—1	EA—1, GB—0	L—0, NW—1	EA—1, GB—0	L—0, NW—1	EA—1, GB—0	L—0, NW—1
Period t_1 (before interest and taxes are paid)								
	EA—0, GB—1.05*	L—0, NW—1.05*	EA—1.05, GB—0	L—.05†, NW—1	EA—1.05, GB—0	L—0, NW—1.05	EA—1.05	L—0, NW—1.05
Period t_1 (after interest and taxes are paid)								
	EA—.05, GB—1	L—0, NW—1.05	EA—1	L—0, NW—1	No transfer necessary			

Symbols: EA—earning assets; GB—government bonds; L—liabilities; NW—net worth; PB—private bonds; PA—public assets.

Assumptions: (1) Neither the capital value of the public project nor the capitalized value of future tax payments is included in individuals' balance sheets. (2) The public project is completely unproductive. (3) The rate of return on private investment is equal to the rate of interest on government securities (5 per cent).

*The .05 represents accrued interest not yet received.

†Accrued liability not yet paid.

Table II

	With Public Debt				Without Public Debt			
	Lender		**Borrower-Taxpayer**		**Lender**		**Borrower-Taxpayer**	
Period t_0 (before debt creation)	EA—1	L—0 NW—1	EA—1	L—0 NW—1	EA—1	L—0 NW—1	EA—1	L—0 NW—1
Period t_0 (after debt creation)	EA—0 GB—1	L—0 NW—1	EA—1	L—0 NW—1	EA—1	L—0 NW—1	EA—1	L—0 NW—1
Period t_1 (before interest is paid)	EA—0 GB—1.05	L—0 NW—1.05	EA—1.10*	L—.05 NW—1.05	EA—1.05	L—0 NW—1.05	EA—1.05	L—0 NW—1.05
Period t_1 (after interest is paid)	EA—.05 GB—1	L—0 NW—1.05	EA—1.05	L—0 NW—1.05	No transfer necessary			

Symbols: EA—earning assets; GB—government bonds; L—liabilities; NW—net worth; PB—private bonds; PA—public assets.

Assumptions: (1) Neither the capital value of the public project nor the capitalized value of future tax payments is included in individuals' balance sheets.
(2) The rate of return on the public project is equal to the rate of return on private investment and to the interest rate on government securities (5 per cent).

*Income from public project assumed to accrue directly as increase in earning assets to taxpayer-borrower.

Table III

	With Public Debt		Without Public Debt	
	Lender	Borrower-Taxpayer	Lender	Borrower-Taxpayer
Period t_0 (before debt creation)	EA—1 | L—0, NW—1	EA—1 | L—0, NW—1	EA—1 | L—0, NW—1	EA—1 | L—0, NW—1
Period t_0 (after debt creation)	EA—0, GB—1 | L—0, NW—1	EA—1 | L—0, NW—1	EA—1 | L—0, NW—1	EA—1 | L—0, NW—1
Period t_1 (before interest is paid)	EA—0, GB—1.05 | L—0, NW—1.05	EA—1.15* | L—.05, NW—1.05	EA—1.05 | L—0, NW—1.05	EA—1.05 | L—0, NW—1.05
Period t_1 (after interest is paid)	EA—.05, GB—1 | L—0, NW—1.05	EA—1.10 | L—0, NW—1.10	No transfer necessary	

Symbols: EA—earning assets; GB—government bonds; L—liabilities; NW—net worth; PB—private bonds; PA—public assets.

Assumptions: (1) Rate of return on public project (10 per cent) is double that on private investment and interest rate on government securities which is 5 per cent. (2) Neither the capital value of the public project nor the capitalized value of future tax payments is included in individuals' balance sheets.

*As in Table II, income from public assets assumed to accrue directly as increase in earning assets to taxpayer-borrower.

Table IV

	With Public Debt				Without Public Debt			
	Lender		Borrower-Taxpayer		Lender		Borrower-Taxpayer	
Period t_0 (before debt creation)	EA—1	L—0 / NW—1	EA—1	L—0 / NW—1	EA—1	L—0 / NW—1	EA—1	L—0 / NW—1
Period t_0 (after debt creation)	EA—0 / GB—1	L—0 / NW—1	EA—1 / PA—1	L—1 / NW—1	EA—1	L—0 / NW—1	EA—1	L—0 / NW—1
Period t_1 (before interest is paid)	EA—0 / GB—1.05	L—0 / NW—1.05	EA—1.05 / PA—1.05	L—1.05 / NW—1.05	EA—1.05	L—0 / NW—1.05	EA—1.05	L—0 / NW—1.05
Period t_1 (after interest is paid)	EA—.05 / GB—1	L—0 / NW—1.05	EA—1.05 / PA—1	L—1 / NW—1.05	No transfer necessary			

Symbols: EA—earning assets; GB—government bonds; L—liabilities; NW—net worth; PB—private bonds; PA—public assets.

Assumptions: (1) Both the capital value of the public project and the capitalized value of future tax payments are fully incorporated in individuals' balance sheets. (2) Rates of yield on public and private investment are equal to each other and to the interest rate on government securities (5 per cent).

Table V

	With Public Debt				With Private Debt			
	Lender		Borrower-Taxpayer		Lender		Borrower-Taxpayer	
Period t_0 (before debt creation)								
	EA—1	L—0 NW—1	EA—1	L—0 NW—1	EA—1	L—0 NW—1	EA—1	L—0 NW—1
Period t_0 (after debt issue)								
	EA—0 GB—1	L—0 NW—1	EA—1 PA—1	L—1 NW—1	EA—0 PB—1	L—0 NW—1	EA—2	L—1 NW—1
Period t_1 (before interest is paid)								
	EA—0 GB—1.05	L—0 NW—1.05	EA—1.05 PA—1.05	L—1.05 NW—1.05	EA—0 PB—1.05	L—0 NW—1.05	EA—2.10	L—1.05 NW—1.05
Period t_1 (after interest transfer)								
	EA—.05 GB—1	L—0 NW—1.05	EA—1.05 PA—1	L—1 NW—1.05	EA—.05 PB—1	L—0 NW—1.05	EA—2.05	L—1 NW—1.05

Symbols: EA—earning assets; GB—government bonds; L—liabilities; NW—net worth; PB—private bonds; PA—public assets.

Assumptions: (1) Both capital value of public investment and capitalized value of future tax payments are fully incorporated in individuals' balance sheets. (2) Rates of yield on public and private projects are equal to each other and to rate of interest on government securities. (3) Alternative to public debt is private debt to finance same project.

Therefore, to arrive at a composite individual balance sheet, the individual's T-account as a bond purchaser must be combined with his account as a taxpayer-borrower. The separation of these two roles does, however, allow us to clarify the analysis, although such separation here should not be taken to mean that the individual may not in many cases fill both roles simultaneously.

6. Internal and
External Public Loans

The third bulwark of the new orthodoxy is perhaps the most vulnerable of the whole structure. This consists in the argument that the external public debt is conceptually distinct in essential and important economic respects from the internal debt. The vulnerability of this proposition is especially evident at this stage following, as it does, the demonstration that the other two sides of the new orthodoxy triangle cannot be supported. From a rather straightforward extension of the arguments developed in the preceding chapters it becomes evident that much of the conceptual difference between the two debt forms disappears. The logic by which we shall establish the converse proposition that internal and external debt are equivalent in many of the important respects is somewhat more direct than that involved in our discussion of the other two propositions. In one sense, therefore, this discussion may be considered as a clarification of what has gone before.

"We Owe It to Ourselves"

Following the procedure of the earlier chapters, we may examine carefully the statements made regarding the internal-external debt distinction. We have already cited Lerner in Chapter 2, but it will be useful to repeat a portion of his argument here.

> One of the most effective ways of clearing up this most serious of all semantic confusions is to point out that private debt differs from national debt in being *external*. It is owed by one person to others. That is what makes it burdensome. Because it is *interpersonal* the proper analogy is not

to national debt but to *international* debt. . . . There is no external creditor. "We owe it to ourselves."[1]

We should also cite Philip E. Taylor:

> To the extent that public debt is held by citizens of the debtor government, "we owe it to ourselves." This is equally true of private debt when viewed in the large. If on the other hand the debt is owed to citizens or governments of other societies, payments on the debt represent deductions from national product, and the standards of national welfare are thereby reduced. This does not mean that funds borrowed from abroad are unproductive to the borrowing economy. It means simply that investment of funds borrowed from abroad produces less net return to the borrowing economy than would similar investment of funds provided at home.[2]

Or, if we prefer to cite more venerable authority, Pigou will suffice:

> It is true that *loans raised from foreigners* entail a burden represented in the interest and sinking fund on future generations in the borrowing country. But interest and sinking fund on *internal* loans are merely transfers from one set of people in the country to another set, so that the two sets together—future generations as a whole—are not burdened at all . . . it is the present generation that pays.[3]

From these statements the implication is clear that, when a community is faced with a choice between the two loan forms, its choice will determine the location of the primary real burden of the debt. If it chooses the external loan, this primary real burden is shifted to "future generations"; if it selects the internal loan, the present generation will bear the sacrifice.[4]

In the analysis of Chapter 4 we showed that the primary real burden is

1. Abba P. Lerner, "The Burden of the National Debt," in Lloyd A. Metzler et al., *Income, Employment and Public Policy* (New York, 1948), p. 256.

2. Philip E. Taylor, *The Economics of Public Finance* (Rev. ed.; New York, 1953), p. 187. Cited by permission, The Macmillan Company.

3. A. C. Pigou, *A Study in Public Finance* (3d ed.; London, 1949), p. 30.

4. For example, Murphy, after arguing that the real costs of war cannot be shifted in time, continues: "There are some exceptions to this generalization. The cost of a war might be financed in part from foreign loans and these loans repaid out of the proceeds of tomorrow's labor." (Henry C. Murphy, *The National Debt in War and Transition* [New York, 1950], p. 80.)

shifted forward even in the case of the internal loan. Thus, in one sense, we have already demonstrated that the distinction between the two loan forms is fallacious. However, in spite of the redundancy and repetitiousness of the analysis, it will be useful to apply the methods directly to the internal-external loan distinction. The basic deficiency in methodology which is common to all aspects of the new orthodoxy comes clearest into light here.

Relevant Alternatives

I shall again assume, only for two paragraphs, the role of an advocate of the currently accepted views.

If a debtor community should be faced with two alternative situations identical in all respects save that in one of these the public debt instruments are internally held while in the other such instruments are externally owned, the first of these alternatives would clearly be preferable. This conclusion would follow whether we conduct our analysis in terms of social aggregates or in terms of individual components. The external debt would require that interest payments be made to foreigners, and such payments would represent deductions from income otherwise disposable. The interest payments on the internal debt represent no such deductions. While taxpayers are no better off, there are now bondholder interest recipients, and the interest payments are mere transfers. The external debt is more burdensome to the community, and to the individuals within it, than an internal debt of comparable magnitude.

This remains true regardless of the relative rates of interest which the two loans might carry. On this logic, the external debt carrying an interest payment of no more than 1 per cent would be more burdensome than an internal debt carrying a rate of 10 per cent. The relative rates of interest do not enter into the argument, and, by implication, into the original choice between the two debt forms. So ends the statement of the ruling conception.

The analysis by which the above conclusions are reached exposes the methodological fallacy already discussed in Chapter 3. Alternatives of the sort mentioned cannot exist either in the real or in the conceptually real world. The relevant comparison for meaningful debt theory is not between two situations which are identical in *every other respect* than debt ownership. Situations like these could never be present, and could never be constructed except as isolated and unimportant cases. Some *other respects* than debt ownership must be different, and any analysis which overlooks or ignores the other necessary differences must embody serious error.

In order to define properly the relevant, and realizable, alternatives, it is necessary to examine these at the moment of initial decision or choice, that is, at the moment when the creation of the public loan is only one among several alternative actions which the community could adopt. In such a moment the community faces three broadly defined alternatives. First, it may borrow and in this way finance a public expenditure program. Secondly, it may tax currently to finance the expenditure, and, thirdly, it may neither borrow, nor tax, nor spend. Inflation of the currency may be construed as a tax for our purposes here. Within each of these broad categories there are, of course, many possible subalternatives. We are concerned here only with those within the first. We shall assume that the community has made the decision to undertake the expenditure and to finance it by the borrowing method. Financing by means of ordinary taxation or by inflation has been ruled out. The only remaining decision concerns the form which the loan shall take.

Shall the government debt instruments be marketed domestically or shall they be sold in foreign countries?

If the first alternative is chosen, and the loan funds are secured from internal sources, the public expenditure project will be financed out of current domestic savings which presumably could have been, and in this model would have been, invested productively in the private domestic economy. Let us disregard for the time being the whole question of the productivity or the unproductivity of the public expenditure project. The creation of the internal public debt will act so as to reduce the community's privately employed capital stock by the amount of the loan. Future private income streams for the community are correspondingly lowered, with the precise amount of such reductions depending on the rate of return on private capital investment.

In the contrary case in which the community chooses to float the public loan externally rather than internally, the public expenditure will be financed from foreign savings. The incremental addition to domestic privately employed capital stock is not affected by the process of public debt creation. Therefore, as compared with the internal loan situation, the private income stream in subsequent time periods is higher. To this higher income stream there must, of course, be attached some drainage sufficient to allow the external loan to be serviced and eventually amortized.

It cannot be overemphasized that the internal and the external debt *cannot* legitimately be compared on the assumption of an equivalent gross income stream in the two cases. The gross income of the community in any chosen future time period cannot be thrown into the *other respects* which are assumed identical in the two cases and thereby neglected. The external debt alternative must allow the community to receive a higher gross income in the future, quite apart from any consideration at all of the productivity of the public expenditure.

Criteria for Choice

Once this simple fact is recognized, the choice between the two debt forms is somewhat more complicated than the new orthodoxy implies. The community must compare one debt form which allows a higher income over future time periods but also involves an external drainage from such income stream with another form which reduces the disposable income over the future but creates no net claims against such income. The choice must hinge on some comparison between the rates at which the required capital sum originally may be borrowed. The choice between the internal and the external loan should, at this level of comparison, depend upon the relative rates at which funds may be secured from the two sources.

The community should be indifferent between the two loan forms if the external borrowing rate is equivalent to the internal borrowing rate, and if we may neglect the frictional or second-order effects of making the interest transfers. This latter neglect obscures important aspects of the problem here, and we shall discuss it at length later, but it is useful to proceed at this stage on the "equal ease of transfer" assumption. We shall temporarily assume that the making of international transfers is no more difficult than the making of internal transfers.

If the two rates are equivalent under these assumptions, the internal loan would reduce domestic private investment which would, in turn, reduce the future income in any one period by an amount indicated by the magnitude of the loan multiplied by the internal rate or net yield on capital, which is assumed to be the rate at which the government borrows. The external loan would not cause such a reduction in private investment; income in a future period would be higher than in the internal loan case by precisely the amount necessary to service the external loan. Net income after all tax payments and interest receipts are included will be equivalent in the two cases.

The analysis is readily extended to the other possible situations. If the internal or domestic productivity of capital investment exceeds the rate at which funds may be borrowed externally, the community will be better off if it chooses the external loan form. Net income after all debt service charges are met will be higher than it would be if the alternative internal public loan were created.

In the third possible case in which the internal rate of return on capital investment falls short of the external borrowing rate, the community will be worse off with the external than with the internal loan. Net income of the community after debt service will be lower, and the external debt will impose a "burden" in a differential sense. But it must be noted that the "burden" imposed by the external debt in this case is no different from that imposed by the internal debt in the converse situation. The differential burden, or pressure, arises, not at all from the locational source of the loan funds, but from the fact that the community has not chosen the most "economic" or "efficient" source. The borrowing operation is not rational in either case, and the differential burden arises from the irrationality in community choice, not from the "externalness" or "internalness" of the debt.

The Transfer Problem

In reaching the above conclusions, we have employed the "equal ease of transfer" assumption. We assumed that the making of internal transfers and international or external transfers are equivalent in effect. This simplifying assumption may appear to remove the fundamental elements of the internal-external debt comparison. That this is not really the case may be illustrated by reference to the problem of state and local debt. Such debts are normally classified as "external." Yet there is no apparent "transfer problem" in the Keynes-Ohlin sense involved in making the interest payments on these obligations. Such interstate and interregional transfers are presumably effected as smoothly as are the purely "internal" transfers required for servicing the internally held national debt. These results stem, of course, from the existence of the common monetary system and the comparatively free resource mobility among the separate regions of the country. For the individual state, the choice between the external and the internal debt should be dictated purely by market criteria.

This illustration should suffice to indicate that the problem of transfer is a second-order one when the distinctions between the external and internal debt are considered. No attempt need be made, and none is made here, to minimize the possible differences in the two cases when the genuinely international debt is compared with the internal debt. But the point is that such differences stem solely from the institutional framework imposed by the separate national monetary and economic structures. There are, of course, differences between the two loan forms when we introduce these institutional problems. But these differences are not the ones which the new orthodoxy has employed in making the external-internal debt distinction. The fact that the external debt involves a drainage out of a domestic income stream is not the reason that the external debt may be burdensome. And this is the clear implication of the new orthodoxy as the earlier citations prove.

Let us now examine the transfer problem in somewhat more detail and see how it might cause us to modify our conclusions reached above. A transfer problem is created by the necessity of servicing either the internal or the external debt. Insofar as the purchase pattern of those taxed to pay the debt interest differs from that of the domestic bondholders in the first case, and from foreigners in the second, some shifting of resources must take place. The issue concerns the differences in the two cases.

Some assumption must be made about exchange rate flexibility. In a world characterized by free flexibility in exchange rates, the international and the internal transfer problems would be substantially identical. For example, if Canada should decide to undertake a large-scale borrowing program, it would make little difference whether the bonds are sold in the United States or at home. The guiding principle in this case should be the comparative rates of interest. Similarly, if the world economy were characterized by some accepted international monetary system with fixed exchange rates, but each economy in the system enjoyed internal price flexibility, the international transfer need be no more difficult than the internal transfer. To be sure, the debtor community will find it necessary to impose domestic deflation in order to surmount the balance-of-payments problems created by the necessity of transferring interest payments abroad. The point to be emphasized here is that the servicing of an internal debt requires that a similar deflationary effect be automatically imposed on the "taxpayer" sector of the domestic economy.[5]

It has been advanced as a conceptual possibility that, either under fixed or flexible exchange rates, extreme values for the elasticities of demand for imports and exports could prevent any transfer of income abroad which is consistent with international equilibrium in balances of payment. Much has been made of this possibility in recent years, but its existence may be questioned.[6] Even if the existence of this possibility is accepted, however, it should be noted that similar extreme values for certain elasticity coefficients in the various sectors of the domestic economy could produce similar results in reference to the internal transfer.

The current world economy is not, of course, characterized by either flexible exchange rates or an international monetary standard. Therefore, certain differential problems are created when "international" loans are considered in this setting. The transfer problem in its classical form may arise, and some premium may be placed on the internal loans. This becomes especially true when the borrowing country obligates itself to service its debt in some international unit of account. In this case, the borrowing or debtor country no longer can retain control over the amount of real income transfer necessitated by the debt service. Action taken in foreign creditor countries can modify the size of the real income transfer.

The point to be made here is not that of minimizing the importance of the transfer problem. Rather it is that of stating that differences in the transfer difficulties provide the only *valid* reason for making a sharp conceptual distinction between the two debt forms. At the more fundamental level of comparison with which we are concerned here, this transfer difference is an adjustment factor only. It should not be allowed to obscure the essential truth, namely, that in basic respects the internal loan and the external loan are identical.

5. Cf. August Lösch, "A New Theory of International Trade," *International Economic Papers,* No. 6, pp. 50–65.

6. See Egon Sohmen, "Demand Elasticities and Foreign Exchange Rates," *Journal of Political Economy,* LXV (1957), 431–36.

Sources of Error

What are the sources of the fallacious idea that the external loan and the internal loan differ in fundamental respects? There appear to be two. The first source of the error is found in the general assumption of the classical economists that all public expenditure is unproductive. If this assumption were true, then the external loan would always make future generations worse off than they would be without the loan. But again the relevant alternative must be considered. Similar conclusions would follow when the internal loan is considered. But the failure to see this may have been based on an oversight of the proper capital-income relationship. With the internal loan, the present value of the community's future income stream is directly reduced because of the direct usage of a portion of its current capital stock in an unproductive manner. This present value is not affected, in the aggregate, by the future interest charges which take the form of internal transfers. But with the external loan, the net present value of the community's income stream is reduced, not by any current using-up of resources, but by the necessity of making the future interest payments. The gross value must be adjusted downward by the present value of the interest payments. This adjustment may not be made explicitly, and, therefore, the external loan may appear to carry with it a greater burden.

The second source of the error lies in the failure of the new economics to make a distinction between the real and the monetary aspects of public debt. The "new" approach to the public debt was related directly to the budgetary aspects of the new economics. Discussion was conducted almost wholly in terms of monetary debt obligations, and little attempt was made to separate the real and the monetary sides of the problem. This aspect of debt theory will be thoroughly discussed in Chapter 9 when we introduce the Keynesian assumptions.

7. Consumption Spending, the Rate of Interest, Relative and Absolute Prices

Having analyzed public debt issue under an initially restricted set of assumptions, it is now appropriate that these assumptions be relaxed and that the effects on the conclusions be examined. It will be useful to proceed in two stages. In this chapter, I shall modify the restrictive assumptions concerning the source of funds, the effects on the rate of interest, and the effects on the structure of prices. The broader assumptions which keep the analysis within the "classical" model will be retained. That is, the analysis will be limited to real-debt issue in periods of substantially full employment. These "classical" assumptions will be dropped in Chapters 9 through 11.

Debt Creation and Consumption Spending

Perhaps the most restrictive of the assumptions was that which stated that all funds utilized in the purchase of government securities are to be drawn from private investment outlay. Even in the case of genuinely "marginal" debt, that is, debt issue small enough so that effects upon the interest rate and relative prices may be neglected, "marginal" sums could be drawn from either private investment, consumption, or both. It will be useful, therefore, to assume that the funds are drawn from current consumption spending while retaining all of the other previous assumptions. We continue to analyze the "classical" model and to assume that the debt is "marginal."

How does this single change in our assumptions affect the three basic propositions put forward at the beginning of Chapter 4? The first of these stated that the primary real burden of public debt is shifted forward in time, and that future taxpayers comprise the group which is differentially affected adversely by debt issue. One of the reasons why this possibility is denied in much of the new orthodoxy seems to lie in the implicit assumption that the funds are drawn from current consumption. Groves states: "If the bonds are sold in that community, it can be argued that the present generation takes the whole cost out of the scale of living it might have had."[1] But whether or not the bond purchaser draws down investment or consumption spending is of no relevance in locating the primary real burden of debt. If the bond purchaser draws down consumption spending there is no indication that he has sacrificed any utility in so doing. In purchasing the bond he is taking advantage of a new opportunity made available to him, and presumably he moves to a more, rather than a less, preferred position. The apparent failure to recognize this rather simple point seems to be in some implicit assumption that the individual must try to maximize current utility rather than a present value of expected utility over time. The rational individual will always try to maximize the latter. In so doing he will set up various trading ratios between current usage of income and wealth accumulation. The fact that he may actually consume less does not indicate that he has moved to a less preferred position on his utility surface.

The second basic proposition, discussed in detail in Chapter 5, stated that the public debt and private debt are analogous in most essential respects. Under the assumption that funds are withdrawn from private investment, the validity of this proposition was quite readily demonstrated, and the converse proposition held by the new orthodoxy was shown to be in error because of the failure to consider the alternative position of the creditor in the no-debt case. The analysis was centered on the fact that this position would be roughly equivalent with or without debt, and from this it was concluded that the offsetting of tax payments against interest receipts is inappropriate. When we change the assumption concerning the source of funds, the analysis becomes a bit more complex, although it remains identical in its essentials. If, when the opportunity to buy government securities is presented, the individual draws down consumption spending rather than his investment spending (directly or indirectly through the purchase of private bonds), his net worth in future time periods will be increased. Through giving up con-

1. Harold M. Groves, *Financing Government* (New York, 1954), p. 561.

sumption goods rather than claims to future private income, the individual increases his net worth in future periods over what it would be had he chosen the alternative sacrifice of private investment. Thus, in the absence of the public debt offering, the individual deliberately chooses to consume currently available real goods and services in the place of future income. It must be recognized, however, that this decision to employ funds in the purchase of consumption goods and services involves some comparison of present values. In this comparison the utility value of real income derived from present usage exceeds the present value of the expected utility derived from the future income stream made possible by private investment. In other words, in the absence of public debt issue, the *opportunity* for private investment exists, and thus the *opportunity* for the potential creditor to increase his net worth over time. His failure to realize this opportunity, rationally or irrationally, does not modify the conclusions reached concerning the analogy between public and private debt. The potential increase in the net worth of the bondholder is present as an available choice among alternatives quite independently of the productivity of the public investment which is debt financed. The modification of the basic assumption to allow for the withdrawal of funds from current consumption spending does nothing toward justifying the "transfer payment" approach to public debt.

We may now re-examine the third proposition in the light of the modified assumptions. Do the internal and the external debts remain fundamentally equivalent? This proposition may appear to be on somewhat weaker ground when we allow funds used in the purchase of government debt instruments to be drawn from consumption spending. The external public loan, drawing its resources solely from foreigners, will not affect directly the domestic consumption-savings pattern. The internal public loan, on the other hand, may draw some resources from current consumption. Insofar as this takes place, internal debt issue does not reduce future incomes gross of interest transfer as much as the external debt reduces future incomes net of interest transfer. The future private income stream under the internal loan compares more favorably with the future private income stream under the external loan than was indicated by the analysis of Chapter 6. If the external and the internal borrowing rates are identical, future income in any particular period will be higher under the internal loan alternative, provided that some portion of the funds is drawn originally from consumption.

It was stated in Chapter 6 that the community should be indifferent between the two loan forms if the domestic rate of productivity on investment is equal to the external borrowing rate, transfer difficulties neglected. If this conclusion must be changed, our proposition to the effect that the two loan forms are fundamentally equivalent must be modified. It seems reasonable to assume that the test for equivalence here should be whether or not some consideration other than ordinary market criteria for choosing between the two loan forms needs to be introduced. But does the fact that future net incomes will be lower under the external debt than under the internal debt lead to an abandonment of the use of market criteria in choosing? The answer is *no*. Closer examination reveals that the ordinary market criteria should be abandoned only if the community desires to place some differential premium on future as opposed to current consumption, some differential other than the negative one indicated by the market rate of exchange. If the market rate of interest is accepted as the most appropriate rate of discount which may be used to bring future incomes into some meaningful comparison with present incomes, the earlier conclusion continues to hold. The community should be indifferent between the two debt forms if the borrowing rates are equal, transfer problems neglected.

The analysis may be clarified by an arithmetical example. Suppose that the government estimates that it can borrow funds internally or externally at a net rate of 5 per cent, which is equal to the net rate of return on domestic private investment. A total loan of $100 is needed. If the government sells its securities externally, it will secure $100 which will carry with it an annual interest charge of $5. If it borrows internally, the rate of current capital formation is not reduced by the full $100 under our modified assumptions. Let us say that $90 will come from previously planned investment whereas $10 will come from new savings which would have gone into consumption outlay but for the debt issue. Future income will be reduced by only $4.50 (5 per cent of $90) while in the external loan case the debt service charge will be $5.00. Net of debt service future income in any one period will be less by 50 cents in the external loan case. However, this annual differential of 50 cents discounts to a present value of precisely $10 if the market rate of 5 per cent is used. Thus, while the internal and the external loan may exert differing effects on the time shape of the community's net income flow, if incomes in the separate time periods are related to each other by the market rate of interest, the present value of the community's income stream at the time the choice between the two loan forms is to be made is the same in each case.

The Rate of Interest

Any sale of securities must, *ceteris paribus,* increase the total supply of "bonds" offered. This increase in supply will tend to exert a depressing influence on price except in two extreme cases. These extreme models may be discussed initially, followed by three additional models which are perhaps more meaningful.

Model 1. If a pure productivity theory of interest rate determination and capital is adopted, the long-run supply curve for bonds is horizontal at a price which reflects the prevailing rate of yield at all of the appropriate margins of investment. Every investment is adjusted so as to provide this rate of yield, and the supply of new savings (demand for new bonds) is so small relative to the total capital stock that this rate of yield is affected negligibly by any change. The issue of additional public "bonds" would not drive the pure rate of yield up, and these bonds could be marketed successfully only through a replacement of private bonds with public bonds. Insofar as this theory of interest rate determination is accepted, the rate of interest (the price of bonds) is unaffected by public debt issue, and the conclusions reached in the preceding chapters of this book hold good without the necessity for the amplifying analysis of this section.[2]

Model 2. On the other hand, if the demand for bonds (the supply of new savings) is infinitely elastic at the prevailing price before debt issue, the increase in the supply of bonds will not act so as to drive prices down and thus interest rates upward. In this particular case, the funds will not be drawn at all from private capital formation but will instead be drawn exclusively from current consumption spending. The analysis of the preceding section holds good here, and the interest rate need not be introduced as a variable. Several peculiarities of this particular extreme model should be noted. The rate of private capital formation not being reduced by the debt issue, future private

2. There is, of course, a fundamental indeterminacy in this model similar to that which occurs in any fully competitive model.

incomes gross of interest charges on the debt are not affected by the debt issue *per se*. Therefore, in this model the ratio between real-debt burden and income in any future period is lower than in other possible cases. The rate of interest does not rise as a result of debt issue, and the government draws none of its funds from private capital formation. In all other cases (including that discussed in the preceding paragraph), either one or both of these happens and the ratio of debt burden to future income is thereby increased.

Model 3. In any meaningful model, the increase in the supply of bonds will exert a depressing influence on price. The effects of the price decrease (rate of yield increase) will depend upon the response on the demand-for-bonds side. We may first consider the case in which the demand is completely unresponsive to the shift in price occasioned by the shift in supply. If this situation is present, that is, if the demand for new bonds is of zero price elasticity (if the supply of new savings is of zero interest elasticity), the analysis of public debt contained in the preceding chapters is not substantially modified. The higher rates of return serve to ration an unchanged supply of new savings among the several borrowers, public and private, with those willing to pay the higher rates, including government, securing the available funds. Submarginal borrowers (at the newly established higher rate) will be eliminated from the market since their bonds will not find takers. Funds secured by the government are secured solely through a withdrawal from private capital formation. It is noted that the primary real-debt burden relative to future incomes is greater in this case than in model 2. First, the current rate of private capital formation is reduced, thus reducing gross private incomes in future time periods. Second, the rate of interest is increased.

The analysis of "marginal" debt issue contained both in earlier chapters and the first section of this chapter demonstrated that no individuals in the economy suffer any reduction in utility when debt is created. When we introduce the variability of the interest rate this conclusion no longer holds true. Those individuals who are disappointed in their borrowing plans, those who are either eliminated from the loan market or who are forced to pay a higher rate for current command over resources as a result of the debt issue, find themselves in a less preferred position than they would be in without the government action.

Can these individuals be said to "bear" a portion of the real burden of the public debt? If the answer is in the affirmative, is not a fundamental thesis of the new orthodoxy re-established, at least to some degree? The answer to this question is that the loss in utility suffered by disappointed borrowers cannot legitimately be defined as a part of the real-debt burden. This loss in utility is offset by some gain in utility enjoyed by lenders. These gains and losses represent secondary repercussions of the government's action in issuing debt. While they cannot be compared in terms of utility, they are in offsetting directions, and in dollar terms may be compared. Conceptually at least, the benefited lenders can overcompensate the disappointed borrowers.[3]

These conclusions may be stated differently. The purchasers of government securities, the lenders, give up precisely enough funds to allow the government to secure the current command over real resources which it desires. Therefore, apart from this primary transfer from private to public employments, the amount of resources remaining for private disposition remains unchanged. No additional net sacrifice is involved in the government's borrowing operation. The disappointed borrowers cannot be said to bear a portion of the real burden of public debt.[4]

---

3. Overcompensation is possible because we are considering the repercussions in this partial sector alone. If further effects are traced, the possibility of overcompensation will, of course, disappear.

4. We may compare this conclusion with the statement made earlier that, in the classical model, inflation can best be considered as a tax. Since the effects of inflation are such as to cause individuals to be confronted with opportunities unfavorable to them which they did not expect, is this not equivalent to the case with the disappointed borrower? The equivalence is only apparent here. In inflation, which is designed to allow government purchase of real goods and services without taxation, the amount of real goods and services available for private disposition is reduced. There are, of course, individuals who gain and individuals who lose by such inflations. But, in net terms, individuals in the aggregate must give up the share of resources which the government, through inflationary finance, purchases.

A second comparison may be drawn between this case and that of a partial excise tax on a particular good. This causes the price of the good to be increased. We say that consumers "bear" the incidence of the tax. Is this not equivalent to the debt case; and may we not say that borrowers forced to pay the higher rates "bear" the burden of the debt? Again the equivalence is only apparent. We say that the consumers or purchasers of the taxed commodity "bear" the tax because they are the only ones in the economy who give up real goods and services in the process of government's action. If the government operation merely increases the retail price of a good, along with the factor prices for resources going into its production, we would not call this shift in relative values a "bur-

Model 4. Although the assumption of zero interest elasticity in the supply of new savings is useful in an introductory model, any serious analysis must also examine the other possible responses.

We may first assume that the supply of new savings increases as the rate of interest increases. This will insure that at least some portion of the funds which go into purchasing debt instruments is drawn from current consumption spending, or, stated more correctly, that the full amount of the public loan is not drawn from private capital formation. The effects of this modification of the analysis have already been discussed. Several points should be noted in addition.

Insofar as the rate of interest rises as a result of the increase in the supply of bonds, this reflects the existence of alternative investment opportunities on the one hand and alternative current consumption opportunities on the other. The degree of shift in the rate of interest measures the real burden of securing the funds from private employments. The magnitude of this burden will vary depending on the change in yield rates, both in investment and consumption, occasioned by the debt issue. And these changes in yield rates are determined, in turn, by the shapes of the relevant investment and consumption aggregate demand functions. There are two reasons why the primary real burden of debt, issued under conditions of a positively sloping supply curve for new savings, will be relatively less oppressive on future generations than that of debt issued under the supply conditions discussed in models 2 and 5. The rate of interest will be increased but not to the degree that it will be in the other cases. And, since some of the funds come from consumption spending, private capital formation and, thus, private incomes in the future are reduced less than in the alternative models.

---

den." The increase in price would have harmed net consumers of the commodity, but it would have benefited net producers. The excise tax differs in that it places a "wedge" between product price and factor price. Government debt issue places no "wedge" between the private lending rate and the private borrowing rate. Its action serves merely to shift the terms of trade between borrowing and lending groups in the economy. These shifts in real income are secondary repercussions which are quite different from the primary real burden which is attributable to the debt itself.

For a discussion of the distinction between the "incidence" of an excise tax and the "horizontal shifts in retail product value," see H. P. B. Jenkins, "Excise-Tax Shifting and Incidence: A Money Flows Approach," *Journal of Political Economy,* LXIII (April, 1955), 125–49.

Model 5. We may now examine the case in which the responsiveness of new savings to a change in the interest rate is negative. Here the increase in rate occasioned by the government's issue of debt will actually reduce the supply of new savings forthcoming. The wealth effect exerts an influence in an opposing direction and must more than outweigh the substitution effect. In this model, the primary real burden of debt imposed on future generations is heaviest, both in a relative and an absolute sense. Since savings are actually reduced, this must mean that private capital formation is reduced by more than the amount of the public loan. Gross private income in future periods is correspondingly lowered. In addition, the upward shift in the interest rate will be greater than in either of the other models.

The introduction of the interest rate as a variable does not affect the conclusions of the previous analysis in any important manner. Interest rate changes do create secondary repercussions throughout the economy. Those individuals desiring to supply current command over resources, lenders, find their terms of trade improved, while those desiring to supply future incomes in exchange for current income, borrowers, find their terms of trade worsened. Such secondary repercussions are, however, separate and apart from the primary burden of debt itself. Secondly, the shifts in the interest rate caused by debt issue reflect the magnitude of the primary real burden. If the rate increases greatly, this is indicative of individual evaluation of alternative investment and consumption opportunities. The level of income for the community in future periods is also a function of the type and degree of response of savings to interest rate changes. This may be summarized by saying that future generations will be better off the more easily the present generation can be induced to postpone the receipt of income. But these modifications, or rather, amplifications, of the analysis do not change the three basic propositions stated at the beginning of Chapter 4.

Relative Prices

Any fiscal operation will affect the structure of relative prices, and debt issue is no exception. If we consider the receipts side of the fiscal transaction alone, the effect will be that of reducing prices in the sectors from which the funds are withdrawn. If public debt replaces private debt, the prices of private bonds and, through this, the prices of privately used capital goods will be reduced.

If public debt replaces consumption spending, consumption goods prices will be reduced.

When debt is issued for real purposes, this reduction in prices will tend to be offset by increases in those sectors supplying goods and services which the government intends to purchase. This is, of course, nothing more than the usual way in which the free price mechanism implements the transfer of resources from one sector of the economy to another. Except in the unusual case in which the government should demand the same goods and services which are given up by those previously spending the alternative private loan or consumption funds, there will be a final shifting in product and service prices as a result of the fiscal operation.

This shifting will entail benefits to some individuals, harm to others. Again these are secondary repercussions of the operation which must be recognized. The benefits and the decrements to welfare are roughly offsetting in total, although here, as before, there should be no implication that any measure in terms of individual utilities is possible.

The Absolute Price Level

We have introduced interest rates and relative prices as variables in the analysis of supramarginal issues of public debt. It is also necessary to examine the effects of such debt on the level of absolute prices. In order first to isolate the effects of debt, *per se,* from those of the combined debt issue–public expenditure fiscal operation, it will be useful to consider the problem in a differential sense. We may assume for this purpose that the relevant alternatives under examination are, first, taxation, and second, debt issue, with the same public expenditure to be financed in either case.

If we consider the receipts side alone, it is obvious that the effects must be deflationary under either of these alternatives. But it is equally obvious that such a one-sided analysis is seriously incomplete and partial. The final effects on the level of absolute prices depend on both the receipts and the spendings side of the government's account.

A combined taxing-spending operation may affect the level of prices. The "balanced-budget multiplier" theorem suggests that an increase in tax-financed public expenditure increases money income, and in the full employment model this increase takes the form of price inflation. This theorem has recently been subjected to such severe criticism that even its directional validity seems open to question. But this is not the place to launch into an extended discussion of this aspect of fiscal theory. We are concerned here solely with the differential effects of debt issue relative to those of taxation. It is perhaps sufficient to state that the "balanced-budget multiplier" effects, if they exist for taxation, exist also for debt issue.

As we have indicated in a previous section, debt issue does tend to increase total wealth, public and private. The nominal amount of money is not reduced, and private people consider the claims to future income represented in government securities to be real wealth. Insofar as their real wealth position affects spending plans, private people will not reduce current spending as much as they will in the taxation situation. If we assume for the moment that the balanced-budget multiplier is zero and can be disregarded, this means that, when debt is issued, because of this wealth effect, private people will not reduce private spending sufficiently to offset the increase in government spending which is debt financed. The differential effect of debt issue is, therefore, to increase the level of prices.

This suggests that any nominal issue of debt, the proceeds of which are employed exclusively in the purchase of real goods and services, carries with it some inflation. In the full employment setting, inflation can be considered as a form of taxation. And taxation places a burden on individuals living at the time of the fiscal action, not during some subsequent period. Therefore, insofar as inflation occurs as a result, debt issue must place some burden on the "current" as opposed to future generations. This burden is, however, to be attributed to the *inflation* which is allowed to occur, not to the debt issue itself. It is misleading to confuse the two as Chapter 10 will demonstrate. That this differential burden is not attributable to real-debt issue may be elaborated. The analysis suggests that debt issue, combined with the public spending program so financed, may be accompanied by inflation. But this conclusion follows only when it is assumed that the *full amount* of the funds collected is utilized to purchase real goods and services. In this case, insofar as *inflation* occurs, the transfer of real resources from the private to the public sector is financed, not by real-debt issue alone, but also by taxation. Any inflationary aspect of debt issue can be readily offset by the sale of sufficient securities to allow a surplus of borrowed funds over expenditures. Through this procedure, the absolute price level may be maintained at a constant level, and all of the debt burden shifted forward. This becomes the model for real-debt issue since it allows us to separate real or pure debt from tax financing in the sharpest sense.

In actuality, nominal debt issue may take many forms, and the form may determine the significance of the differential inflationary impact discussed here. If debt instruments are issued which closely resemble money in those characteristics which affect behavior, there will be a sizeable differential impact. The more nearly the debt form approaches money, the further it departs from pure debt. The issue of any particular form of debt which possesses "moneyness" must, in the full employment setting, be considered as some combination of real-debt issue and taxation (inflation). Consider an example. Suppose that the government in 1958 decides to finance a new highway program calling for $1 billion in new spending and to finance this from the sale of Series E Savings Bonds. This billion dollars worth of apparent debt can best be broken down into two parts, real (or pure) debt, and taxation. Suppose, on the other hand, the decision is to finance the same project by pure-debt issue, although still with the Series E form. In this case the government might well find it necessary to issue $1.2 billion, spending the billion for real goods and services and sterilizing the $200 million.

Since any particular form of nominal debt issue can be analyzed in this fashion, it will not be necessary to discuss in detail the differing characteristics of the various debt forms. As these lose "moneyness," that is, as they move along the spectrum from currency toward consols, the proportion of real debt contained in any nominal issue increases, although even consols cannot be considered wholly as pure debt.[5]

It seems essential for clarity in thought and analysis that debt be sharply distinguished from taxation. This distinction is important even in the full employment model, as we have indicated. It becomes more important when we go on to consider other models in later chapters.

5. See the Appendix for a fuller discussion of the points made in this paragraph.

8. A Review of
Pre-Keynesian Debt Theory

This essay has been organized as a critique of the currently orthodox conception of public debt. The analysis lends support to the so-called "vulgar" or "common-sense" ideas on public debt, but, more significantly, it also reestablishes, in large part, the validity of the public debt theory which was widely, although by no means universally, accepted by scholars prior to the Keynesian "revolution" in economic thought. Although I shall make no attempt to include anything approaching a complete doctrinal history, the essay would be seriously incomplete, and it would, perhaps, convey an unintended and false impression of "newness" or "originality" if it did not include specific reference to the earlier literature.

As was indicated in Chapter 3, the conception of public debt which has been labeled the "new orthodoxy" is not new. It is, in fact, very old; for this was the commonly accepted view during the eighteenth century, and, to the "classical" writers, the ideas represented merely a part of the larger body of mercantilist doctrine. It is somewhat singular that these eighteenth-century ideas on public debts were called "common" or "vulgar" by the classical writers. Public debt theory has turned full circle.

David Hume was one of the first English writers to address himself specifically to the subject of public credit. His whole discussion represents an attack on what he calls the "modern" maxim that the "public is no weaker upon account of its debts; since they are mostly due among ourselves, and bring as much property as they take from another."[1] Hume categorically re-

---

1. David Hume, "Of Public Credit," *Essays Moral, Political and Literary,* Vol. I (New ed.; London, 1882), p. 366. Original edition published in 1742.

jected this line of reasoning, claiming that it was a result of "specious comparisons" and not based upon "principles."

Adam Smith devoted forty pages of *The Wealth of Nations* to the public debt.[2] He dismissed the transfer-payment argument as an "apology founded altogether on the sophistry of the mercantile system."[3] But perhaps the most important insight of Smith lies in his clear recognition that the bond purchaser undergoes no sacrifice when the debt is created:

> By lending money to government, they do not even for a moment diminish their ability to carry on their trade and manufactures. On the contrary, they commonly augment it. . . . The merchant or monied man makes money by lending money to government, and instead of diminishing, increases his trading capital.[4]

This statement is nothing more than an elemental recognition of the mutuality of advantage from voluntary exchange, but it is important because this is precisely the point which the holders of the currently orthodox views on public debts have consistently overlooked.

As we have already seen, Ricardo lent some support to the currently orthodox view that interest payments, being in the nature of internal transfers, involve no primary burden. This idea was, in fact, based upon his assumption that future tax payments would be fully capitalized in a world of rational individuals. If taxpayers living during the period of debt creation fully capitalize future tax payments, the interest payments do become mere transfers which involve no "sacrifice" on the part of future generations. Thus, public debt does not shift the real cost of government expenditure forward in time. "The argument of charging posterity with the interest of our debt, or of relieving them from a portion of such interest, is often used by otherwise well informed people, but we confess to see no weight in it."[5]

Ricardo did not, however, swing all the way to the mercantilist position and argue that public debt creation was in the social interest. Hume, Smith,

---

2. Adam Smith, *The Wealth of Nations* (Modern Library Edition; New York, 1937), pp. 859–900.

3. Ibid., p. 879.

4. Ibid., p. 863.

5. David Ricardo, "Funding System," *Works and Correspondence*, P. Sraffa, ed. (Cambridge: Royal Economic Society, 1951), Vol. IV, p. 187.

and Ricardo were in agreement in predicting the consequences of public loans. Their attitudes on this point stemmed from their implicit assumptions concerning the usage to which governments would put revenues. All government expenditure was considered to be wasteful and unproductive; therefore, the real evil of public debt lay in the destruction of capital which it facilitated, not in the debt itself. Thus, we find this group of writers condemning public debt for reason of the public expenditures which it finances as opposed to the post-Keynesian writers who praise debt issue for the same reason. Both groups are equally in error; both fail to separate the two distinct aspects of the fiscal operation; the securing of the funds and the spending of them.

A "classical" theory of the public debt was not provided by the English classical economists. The views of Smith, which were perhaps closest to being the correct ones despite his predilection against debt issue, were never wholly accepted. Ricardo confused the whole argument by his highly abstract model which appeared to contain elements of the earlier mercantilist views. And the third major figure among the English classical economists was hopelessly confused. J. S. Mill, apparently much influenced by the ideas of Chalmers, tried to combine elements of contrasting views. This led him to claim that the public debt has a double burden, one which is borne by the current generation of laborers because resources which would otherwise be used to support labor are withdrawn from private employments, and one which is shifted forward to future generations because of the taxes required for the interest payments.[6]

The "classical" formulation of public debt theory took shape only in the last two decades of the nineteenth century. By this time, the extreme views of the earlier writers on the wastefulness of public expenditures had been sufficiently modified to allow a judicious and careful analysis to be constructed. Also, the world economic situation was such that there arose no great popular or academic clamor for economic policies based on mercantilist ideas of an earlier epoch. It is useful to emphasize, however, that a complete intellectual victory for classical views on public debts was never really achieved. Perhaps even more than in other areas of economic policy discussion, earlier ideas continued to exist side by side with the newer ones. This dichotomy

---

6. J. S. Mill, *Principles of Political Economy* (Ashley Edition; London, 1915), p. 873.

was not clarified by Ricardo's influence since his work seemed to represent both views.

The classical formulation is best represented in the works of H. C. Adams, C. F. Bastable, and P. Leroy-Beaulieu. Their works remain today the most careful analyses of public debts in the literature. The work of H. C. Adams in the United States does not quite measure up to that of Bastable in analytical clarity while that of Bastable remains somewhat below that of Leroy-Beaulieu. By confining any detailed discussion to these three writers, a more incisive statement of the classical position may be conveyed.

Adams was quite clear in his recognition that debt creation *per se* involves no sacrifice on the part of lenders. "A loan calls for no immediate payment from the people. . . . the lenders are satisfied, since they have secured a good investment."[7] His refutation of the argument that the burden of expenditure cannot be shifted forward in time warrants reasonably complete citation:

> . . . there are writers of respectability . . . who deny the inability of a people to meet within the year all necessary expenditures, and who refuse to assent to the time-honored argument that by a loan the burden of a war may be distributed. Such writers claim that the generation engaged in the contest must bear the burden of its expenses, that this burden can in no manner be bequeathed; but that, if the war entail a debt upon the following generations, its burden is borne twice—once by the fathers who furnished the capital that was destroyed, and once by the sons who furnished the money to expunge the debt. Although this latter conception of war expenditure does not appear to me to be quite accurate, it is yet based upon the manifest truth that each generation must subsist upon the product of its own industry. No father can eat the potatoes to be hoed by an unborn son, nor can any army live on bread to be delivered, at the option of the baker, between ten and forty years from the date of the contract. . . .
>
> Such a statement of truisms, however, is no final argument in favor of the taxing policy, nor does it meet fairly the claim of those who say that by means of loans the burden of a conflict may in part be thrown upon posterity . . . *they fail to understand the difference between capital expended in a war and the burden entailed upon the citizens* of a country by a war. The

---

7. H. C. Adams, *Public Debts* (New York, 1893), p. 24. Citations by permission Appleton-Century-Crofts.

consumption of capital may or may not give rise to the consciousness of extraordinary expenditure on the part of the state, according as it does or does not effect *involuntary privation.* The real burden of a war consists in the fact that men are deprived of property without the compensation of hope. In the second place—and here lies the kernel of the argument— they fail to perceive that the most important factor for the financier is not the material but the psychological factor.[8] (Italics supplied.)

The work of C. F. Bastable is somewhat more adaptable to the organization of this essay since he makes reference to each of the three basic propositions which we have classified as essential to the new orthodoxy. Bastable hardly felt it necessary to spell out the shiftability of the debt burden to future taxpayers. The distinction between the loan and the tax is clearly drawn. "A loan is voluntary, and supplied by willing givers; taxation is levied on the willing and the unwilling alike. . . . To make things smooth for the present at the cost of the future is not the duty of the wise and far-seeing statesman."[9]

The false analogy claims were also summarily dealt with. "In all essential points the analogy between the public and private debtor does hold good and should never be lost sight of."[10] The transfer or right-hand–left-hand argument "rests on the same ground as certain views about expenditure and taxation already rejected. The action of indebtedness on the economic system cannot be altogether without influence or effect."[11] "The peculiar position of the state economy and the great importance of public borrowing have both tended to obscure the fundamental truth that public credit is but one form of credit in general, and is, or ought to be, regulated by the same leading principles."[12]

The limitations on the internal-external loan distinction were clearly perceived.

> The fact that a good deal of the funds obtained by public borrowing are derived from abroad is of some weight in judging loan policy. Not that a foreign loan is in its purely financial bearings so different from a home

8. Ibid., pp. 106–7.
9. C. F. Bastable, *Public Finance* (2d ed.; London, 1895), pp. 624–25. Citations by permission Macmillan and Co., Ltd.
10. Ibid., p. 614.
11. Ibid., p. 613.
12. Ibid., p. 609.

one as is sometimes supposed, but that the possibility of drawing on the capital of other countries weakens the argument in favor of taxation on the ground that in any event the expenditures must be met from the national resources.

... from a purely financial point of view the source of a loan is really immaterial. In any case it is an immediate relief to the taxpayer counterbalanced by greater charge in the future.[13]

It is, however, to Paul Leroy-Beaulieu that credit must be given for the most concise and careful analysis of the nature of public debts. Many of the specific points made earlier in this essay are to be found in his treatment, which has been largely overlooked, at least by the English-language scholars. Leroy-Beaulieu begins his analysis by a careful consideration of the contrasting views of the eighteenth-century writers (Melon, Voltaire, Condorcet) and those of the English classical economists. He recognizes that both the extreme views are partially erroneous. The public loan is, in and of itself, neither a good nor an evil. The classical economists are criticized for their failure to recognize that public expenditures can be productive. But the main part of his argument is devoted to a refutation of the eighteenth-century ideas, which Leroy-Beaulieu considers to be not only false but dangerous. He classifies these ideas, which are those of the current orthodoxy, as sophisms which have the appearance of truth, and which persons not versed in economics find difficulty in refuting.[14]

Leroy-Beaulieu's work on public debt theory has not, to my knowledge, been translated into English. This provides an added reason why a somewhat lengthy citation seems appropriate at this point. The translation is my own.

> The sophisms, in regard to public loans, have been presented in many forms, but there are two main ones which we have already indicated: A State which is indebted only to itself is not impoverished, says Voltaire; public debts, writes Melon, are the debts which the right hand owes to the left hand: the right hand here being the contributor, the left hand, the rentier: but it is of little importance for the prosperity of the State whether

13. Ibid., pp. 629–30.
14. Paul Leroy-Beaulieu, *Traité de la Science des Finances* (7th ed.; Paris, 1906), Vol. II, pp. 224–26. Citation by permission Presses Universitaires de France.

this sum of money belongs to the rentier or to the contributor: the nation is equally rich in the two cases.

The fallacy of these sophisms may be demonstrated as follows: It is very true that one of the consequences of public loans is the levying upon contributors by means of a tax a certain sum which is subsequently distributed to the rentiers as interest. If this superficial view is maintained, it could be said that the state is indifferent, that there is no reduction in the public fortune, because certain citizens, under the name of rentiers, receive that paid by other citizens, under the name of contributors or taxpayers. These latter may be pitied, but the nation will not be impoverished. But it is necessary to extend this analysis further. Let us suppose that there had been no loan. The contributors would have retained for themselves the increased tax which is now destined to pay interest to the rentiers. On the other side, the rentiers would have in their possession the capital which they loan to the state in the case of the public loan, and whether they invest this themselves or lend it to entrepreneurs or to industrialists, they would have received an interest approximately equal to that which the state agrees to pay when it creates the debt. Thus, in the case where a public loan is contracted, the rentiers only gain the interest on the capital loaned to the state at the expense of the contributors who pay the taxes. In the case where the loan is not made, the contributors retain the money which they would have had to pay in increased taxes, in order to service the loan. The rentiers, having conserved in their own hands and having invested the capital which they would have loaned to the state otherwise, are not deprived of their interest. One sees the difference in the two cases: When there is a loan, one of the parties is injured; when there is no loan, each of the two parties, the contributor and the rentier, has for his disposition the sum which, in the loan case, would only belong to one of them. To utilize again the image of Melon, when there is a loan, the right hand, that is to say, the contributor, passes his money to the left hand, that is, the rentier. When there is no loan, each of the two hands remains full; no one is dispossessed of anything, and this position is clearly to be preferred.

We have said that a loan has for its object the securing of disposition over outside capital by means of accepting an obligation to pay the interest and sometimes also to pay off the loan at a fixed date. This operation is, in itself, perfectly innocent. It will be useful or it will be harmful according to the employment of the capital which will be made by the borrower who will be assured of the possession of the capital and subsequently the sacrifices which it will be obliged to impose upon itself in order to pay the interest and to amortize the loan. If the borrowing unit employs this sum in a productive manner, in public works, for example (since this is almost the only form in which capital borrowed by the state can be preserved), if it invests in railroads, in canals, in ports, in schools, and if, in addition, investments in these enterprises are made carefully, it is probable that the society will not suffer any detriment by the fact of the public loan. It is even possible that it will prove to be a great benefit if the public works have been judiciously conceived and executed with economy. Because then the society will be deprived of a capital which the rentier will have given up, but this will be transformed into another sort, that of a railroad, a canal, or a port from which the taxpayers will profit. If, on the contrary, the capital which a state has borrowed and from which the rentier is separated, is wasted in the pleasures of the court, in ostentatious buildings, or in foolish enterprises, then it is clear that the society will be impoverished, because the capital which the rentier will have given up will have absolutely ceased to exist, or it will only be represented in unproductive works, such as palaces and jewels.

A loan will be useful or harmful to the society in general depending on whether the state preserves and usefully employs the proceeds, or wastes and destroys the capital which the rentiers have given up. In the past, the passions of sovereigns and the mistakes of governments have had for an effect the disbursing of the greater part of the proceeds of public loans for useless expenditures. This has led many to condemn public credit absolutely, as an instrument of evil. This conclusion is exaggerated. It is as much as to say that it would be desirable for a man to be without sense because he often does not use it properly.[15]

All of the essential elements of the classical theory of public debt are contained in the above citation. Leroy-Beaulieu was careful to avoid the two major errors to be found in other treatments. First of all, he separated the effects

15. Ibid., pp. 226–29.

of the debt creation from those of the public expenditure financed. The failure to accomplish this conceptual separation led the English classical economists to condemn debts erroneously just as it led both the late mercantilists and the neo-Keynesians to applaud debts unduly. Secondly, and this error is also fundamental to the first one, Leroy-Beaulieu's analysis was properly conceived in terms of relevant alternatives. He did not compare the public debt with no debt, *ceteris paribus.* He went back to the initial period when choice among alternatives is possible, and then he compared what would happen with and without the loan.

There is, in fact, little that may be added to the discussion of Leroy-Beaulieu. In a sense, this essay represents an elaboration and an extension of his theory of public debt, although, as is perhaps usual in such cases, I did not fully appreciate or fully discover Leroy-Beaulieu's work until after my own critique of the new orthodoxy had been substantially completed.

The central ideas contained in Leroy-Beaulieu's approach appear to have been widely accepted up until World War I and even into the decade of the 1920's. In his 1917 paper on war finance, O. M. W. Sprague adopts the classical position, but, somewhat similar to the Ricardo case, this is not evident except on a careful reading. And, taken out of context, some of Sprague's statements seem to lend support to the new orthodoxy.[16]

In the period between World War I and the Great Depression the most important work in public debt theory is represented in the report of the Colwyn Committee in 1927.[17] It is difficult to criticize the statements which are made in the Majority Report, because, by and large, these are carefully qualified. There is, however, a certain ambiguity present. In reading the report, one gets the impression that the committee was impressed by both of the contrasting arguments and attempted to incorporate both into its own statement.

> The loss to the nation was, of course, due to the expenditure, and not to the particular method of financing it. The burden of expenditure was incurred once and for all by the nation as a whole: so far as it was met by

16. O. M. W. Sprague, "Loans and Taxes in War Finance," *American Economic Review, Proceedings,* 1917. Reprinted in *Readings in Fiscal Policy* (Homewood, Ill., 1955), pp. 107–21. See especially pp. 113–14.

17. *Report of the Committee on National Debt and Taxation* (London, 1927).

taxation, it was immediately shared out between individual citizens; so far as it was met by internal War Loans, the tax burden on the individual was postponed, the subscriber receiving a claim to future goods and services— in exchange for his money—a claim which could only be met by future taxation on himself and his fellow citizens. The loan entailed a subsequent transfer of wealth within the community for payment of interest and re-payment of capital. This transfer, which is the burden to be attributed to the internal debt itself—as distinct from the war expenditure behind it— does not destroy wealth: it merely redistributes wealth within the com-munity.[18]

Public debt theory had already begun its retrogression from the high point attained in the work of Leroy-Beaulieu. And the Minority Report accepted almost all the basic points later made by the new orthodoxy.[19]

The classical formulation had never achieved a mastery of the field. Both scholars and lay publicists continued to put forward the propositions which Adams, Bastable, and Leroy-Beaulieu had effectively demolished. The onset of the Great Depression and the shift in thought which it engendered, in-cluding the doctrines of Lord Keynes, provided a golden opportunity for these discredited, but never wholly dead, propositions to be revived. New life was pumped into them, and for the first time in two centuries they became respectable.

Appendix: Public Loans Versus Extraordinary Taxes: The Italian Debate

The theory of public debt has occupied an important position in Italian fiscal theory. The contribution of the Italians is sufficiently unique, both in ap-proach and analysis, to warrant special discussion. The theory has been de-veloped almost wholly in terms of the basic Ricardian proposition concern-ing the fundamental equivalence between extraordinary taxes and public loans. This proposition has been discussed at such greater length in Italian works that it may be properly said to belong to the Italian rather than to the English tradition. Since details of doctrinal history are not important for this

18. Ibid., pp. 27–28.
19. Ibid., pp. 358–59.

book, the specific argument which follows may be limited to the main contributors.[20]

The Ricardian thesis, which was elaborated and extended by de Viti de
Marco, has been briefly discussed in Chapter 4, but it may be reviewed again.[21]

It is argued that the fully rational individual should be indifferent between
paying a tax of $2,000 once-and-for-all and paying an annual tax of $100 in
perpetuity, assuming an interest rate of 5 per cent. The analysis is then extended to apply to all individuals, and it is concluded that if the government
borrows $2,000 and thereby commits taxpayers to finance interest payments
of $100 annually, the effects are no different from the levy of an extraordinary
tax of $2,000. In each case individuals living in future time periods will be in
identical positions. The individual living during the time that the expenditure decision is made will fully capitalize all future tax payments, and he will
write down the value of the income-earning assets which he owns by the
amount of the present value of these future payments.

The limited life span of the individual does not affect the analysis. If an
individual pays the once-and-for-all tax, his heirs will receive capital assets
reduced in value by this amount. If, on the other hand, the debt is created,
his heirs will receive capital assets yielding a higher gross income. But when
the interest charge is deducted, the net income stream is equivalent to that
received in the tax situation.

The analysis would, at first glance, appear to apply only to those individ-

20. These are de Viti de Marco and Griziotti. Other works which should be mentioned
are Maffeo Pantaleoni, "Imposta e debito in riguardo alla loro pressione," *Giornale degli
economisti* (1891), reprinted in *Scritti varii di Economia*, Serie Terza (Rome, 1910), pp. 301–
22; "Fenomeni economia delle guerra," *Giornale degli economisti* (1916), pp. 201–3; Luigi
Einaudi, *Miti e paradossi della giustizia tributaria* (Turin, 1938), Ch. 5; Giannino Parravicini, "Debito pubblico, reddito, occupazione," *Rivista di diritto finanziario e scienza delle
finanze* (1951), pp. 25–38; F. Maffezzoni, "Ancora della diversa pressione tributaria del
prestito e dell' imposta," *Rivista di diritto finanziario e scienza delle finanze* (1950), pp. 341–
75; Cesare Brasca, "Intorno agli effetti economici del debito pubblico," *Rivista internazionale di scienze sociale*, XXV (1954), pp. 417–46.

21. The most complete statement of Ricardo's position is to be found in "Principles of
Political Economy and Taxation," *Works and Correspondence*, P. Sraffa, ed. (Cambridge:
Royal Economic Society, 1951), Vol. I, pp. 244–46. De Viti de Marco's elaboration of Ricardo's theory was first published as "La pressione tributaria dell' imposta e del prestito,"
Giornale degli economisti (1893), pp. 38–67, 216–31, but essentially the same analysis is
contained in *First Principles of Public Finance*. Translated by E. Marget (New York, 1938),
pp. 377–98.

uals possessing patrimony or capital. Its extension to other individuals, members of professional or laboring groups, who own no income-earning assets is not initially apparent. But both Ricardo and de Viti de Marco anticipated this objection and attempted to overcome it. The individual who possesses no capital assets which he can sell to raise funds to meet his tax obligation must, through necessity, borrow privately, thereby obligating himself to meet future interest charges on a private debt. In this case, provided only that the interest rate on the public and private debts is the same, the individual owes the same interest charges in each future income period. The effect of the government's replacing the tax with the public loan is nothing more than the replacement of a whole set of private loans with a single public loan.

The basic proposition does show that the extraordinary tax and the loan are fundamentally equivalent. It is in their attempts to extend the conclusions beyond this that both Ricardo and de Viti de Marco became confused. Both of them suggested that the analysis reveals that the public loan does not differentially place a burden on future generations, that this burden in either case rests solely with the individuals living at the time of the initial decision.

Before the question concerning the location of the burden of the debt can be examined, the meaning of "burden" must be examined. If the location of this burden on current generations is to be explained by the full capitalization of all future tax payments, the analysis is consistent with that developed in this book, and the whole issue becomes that of determining whether individuals do, in fact, capitalize future taxes. In this case even if the present generation bears the burden through a reduction in the capital value of their assets owned, it is the future interest charges which represent the weight of the debt. The discounting process merely serves to shift the burden of these *interest* payments backward in time. The process does not eliminate the burden of the interest item in any way. Ricardo argued, however, that the payment of interest did not involve a burden; instead he suggested that the real burden of the public debt is best represented in the initial destruction of capital occasioned by the "profuse expenditure of government." In this way, Ricardo commits the second of the methodological errors discussed in Chapter 3; he confuses the effects of debt issue with the effects of the expenditure which it finances. The productivity or unproductivity of the public expenditure is irrelevant for determining the location of debt burden; this is represented by the interest charges. And the argument reduces to that of determining whether or not these are capitalized.

De Viti de Marco was more careful, and his analysis does not follow Ricardo (and the new orthodoxy) in suggesting that since capital is destroyed in the initial period the debt burden must rest with individuals living in that period. His argument consists in showing that the discounting does, in fact, take place. Even if it is accepted, however, that all individuals owning capital assets or receiving sufficient current income to allow them to contract private loans do fully discount future taxes, there still may be other large groups of individuals. These latter comprise the bulk of the lower income or laboring classes. It is impossible to levy extraordinary taxes upon them which will be drawn from capital formation or property. Such a tax can only be levied on the first two groups. If the public debt is created, on the other hand, some portion of the annual interest charges may be financed from taxes levied upon this third group. The lower income classes in future time periods may bear a portion of the burden of the public loan whereas they must, by definition, escape fully the burden of the extraordinary tax. This is the objection which Griziotti raised to the de Viti elaboration of the Ricardian thesis.[22]

De Viti de Marco attempted to refute this objection, but he was not really successful. He tried to show that even the complete exemption of all nonpropertied individuals from the extraordinary tax would not affect his conclusions. Here he introduced a long-run competitive model. He reasoned that such an exemption would tend to increase the relative attractiveness of the professional nonpropertied occupations. This would, in turn, cause more people to enter these occupations, and to turn away from those activities such as the management and the administration of property. In the long run, the lot of the nonpropertied classes would tend to be identical with that which they would have enjoyed had they been taxed. As Griziotti suggested, this stretching of the competitive model to the equalization of returns among the separate productive factors is going a bit too far. Griziotti's objection cannot be dismissed as introducing a mere distributional consideration which is

22. Benvenuto Griziotti, "La diversa pressione tributaria del prestito e dell' imposta," *Giornale degli economisti* (1917). Reprinted in *Studi de scienza delle finanze e diritto finanziario* (Milan, 1956), pp. 193–261.

not a part of the more abstract model. To be sure, the objection holds only insofar as the actual distribution of the burden of the extraordinary tax differs from that of the debt. But Griziotti's whole point is that the two financing forms themselves must involve different distributions of the burden among income classes, and because of this, among separate time periods.

Griziotti also questioned the basic assumption that individuals, even those owning capital assets, discount future tax payments. Individuals do not act as if they live forever, and family lines are not treated as being continuous. There is nothing sacred about maintaining capital intact, and individuals will not necessarily do so. The equivalence hypothesis requires continued abstinence from consuming capital on the part of those holding assets after public debt is created. Whereas the extraordinary tax effectively removes from an individual's possibilities the capital sum (once he has paid the tax, he can no longer convert this portion of his capital into income), the disposition over this capital remains in his power in the public loan case. He may convert this capital into income at any time, without in any way removing the tax obligation on his heirs which is necessitated by the debt service.

Griziotti's claim that the creation of public debts does involve a shifting of the financial burden forward in time was not successful in overcoming the dominance of the de Viti de Marco elaboration of the Ricardian thesis in Italy. The prestige and apparent logical clarity of the de Vitian argument were successful in reducing the Griziotti influence. There have been isolated supporters of Griziotti,[23] but the de Viti formulation continues to dominate the Italian scene. The argument of Griziotti is, of course, closer to that developed in this essay than is the opposing one.

Additional elements of the de Viti de Marco conception of public debt may be mentioned since he anticipated much of the new orthodoxy. To anticipate erroneous ideas is, of course, no great contribution, but de Viti's arguments concerning the problem of debt repayment are surprisingly modern in this respect. Included in his discussion of the public debt is what he called the theory of automatic amortization. de Viti used this to demonstrate that debt should never be repaid. His construction is worth discussing here because it illustrates yet another failure to consider relevant alternatives.

23. For example, see F. Maffezzoni, "Ancora della diversa pressione tributaria del prestito e dell' imposta," *Rivista di diritto finanziario e scienza delle finanze* (1950), pp. 341–75.

De Viti started from his interpretation of the Ricardian argument that public debt merely serves as a substitute for private debts. He assumes a community of three individuals, only one of whom is a capitalist.[24] Now assume that the state requires a sum of 1,200,000 and levies an extraordinary tax, 400,000 on each individual. Individual 1 being the capitalist, individuals 2 and 3 will find it necessary to borrow from him in order to meet their tax obligations, paying an assumed interest rate of 5 per cent. As these individuals save in future periods, they may amortize their debt to the capitalist.

Now assume that the government, instead of levying the tax, borrows the 1,200,000 directly from Individual 1. The annual interest charge will be 60,000, and it is assumed to collect 20,000 from each of the three citizens. As in the first case, as individuals 2 and 3 save, they may utilize this savings to purchase the government securities, which are assumed to be marketable, from Individual 1. Their purchase of government securities in this case is identical in effect to their paying off private debts in the other case. Therefore, as the government securities are widely circulated among the population the real debt is more or less automatically amortized. Individuals, in purchasing debt instruments, acquire an asset to offset their tax liabilities. The weight of the debt is effectively destroyed; hence debt need never be repaid and there need be no fear that a country cannot bear the burden of public debts, however heavy these might appear to be.

This construction is both ingenious and misleading. Let us consider the private borrowing case carefully. Individuals 2 and 3, as they accumulate savings, increase their net worth, and they must also increase some item on the asset side, let us say, cash. When they accumulate sufficient cash to warrant paying off a portion of the private debt, the transaction is represented on their balance sheets as a drawing down of the cash item and a corresponding drawing down of their liability item. *Net worth does not change with debt repayment.*[25]

The construction is identical with the public loan. As individuals accumulate savings these must take some form, such as cash or savings accounts. Net worth is increased along with whatever asset item the individual chooses

---

24. This argument is developed in his *First Principles of Public Finance*, pp. 390–93.

25. Cf. F. Maffezzoni, "Ancora della diversa pressione tributaria del prestito e dell' imposta," op. cit., p. 348.

to put his savings into. At one point we assume that the individual accumulates sufficient funds to purchase a debt instrument. In so doing, he reduces his cash item and increases another asset item, government securities. He has, in this particular transaction, merely transformed one asset into another. *His net worth is not modified.* Therefore, the weight of having to pay the annual tax upon the debt instrument is precisely as heavy after as before his acquisition of the security.

De Viti de Marco is correct, in the extremes of his model, in saying that this transaction is equivalent to the repayment of private loans. In this sense the *public* debt may be said to be amortized. But his error lies in inferring from this that public debt should not be repaid in fact. This error is the same that we have discussed in Chapter 5. It is based upon a misunderstanding of private loans. Implicit in the de Viti formulation is the idea that the repayment of private loans is necessarily beneficial to the individual. de Viti assumed that such repayment increases private net worth, and thereby reduces the weight or "pressure" of the loan. He failed to see that the new savings which go into private debt repayment have alternative employments. Whether or not private debt repayment reduces "pressure" on the individual economy depends solely upon the relative rates of return.

The same is true for public debt. Having demonstrated that the transfer of public debt instruments might be similar in some models to private debt repayment, de Viti inferred that this "amortization" reduces the pressure or weight of the public debt. This is not necessarily true at all. The weight of debt remains as it was before, and the purchase of government securities can modify this only insofar as the relative rates of yield on government securities and other assets place the individual in a more preferred position.

This demonstration that the de Viti argument does not show that public debt should not be repaid cannot be applied in reverse. By saying that de Viti de Marco was wrong in making this extension is not to say that public debt *should be repaid.* The argument of this essay will be turned to this problem in Chapter 13.

9. Public Debt and Depression

The three fundamental propositions of the currently accepted theory or conception of public debt have been demonstrated to be false and insupportable within the framework of the classical assumptions. The discussion should prove sufficient to destroy any claims that the "transfer payment" approach provides a "general" theory. But is the new orthodoxy not acceptable when the classical assumptions are dropped? And, by implication, does not the classical reformulation fail to apply in conditions of economic depression? Is there one theory of public debt which is appropriate under the classical assumptions and another which is applicable when "Keynesian" conditions prevail?

In this chapter I shall show that there is only one "correct" theory of public debt, and that the reformulation of classical theory developed in this book does provide a "general" theory which is applicable to all possible situations, and under all sets of assumptions. There is no need for two contrasting theories of public debt.

The important difference between the classical and the Keynesian models lies, of course, in the assumption concerning the level of employment. The full employment assumption will now be relaxed, and it is here assumed explicitly that there exist in the economy some economic resources which are not employed at the time of debt creation.

The importance of the two methodological principles discussed in Chapter 3 is worth re-emphasizing. First of all, the necessity of introducing and examining the necessary offsetting or compensating changes in the other fiscal variables cannot be neglected or assumed not to take place. Relevant alternatives must be compared. Secondly, although the compensating changes must be examined as an integral part of the analysis, the two sides of the transaction must be conceptually distinct. Debt theory has been characterized throughout its history by an oversight of both of these principles.

In the classical model it is necessary to distinguish between the real and the monetary aspects of a government borrowing operation only in a secondary sense. The existence of a money economy does not seriously modify the real nature of the transaction involved. Roughly similar conclusions would be produced from an analysis which assumes a pure barter economy. The government borrows resources, either directly or indirectly, through the medium of some generally accepted item classified as money which, in turn, gives to the government command over the disposition of resources. The resources which are transferred to government, via the debt operation, would have been used by private people had not the transfer taken place. In return for these resources, the government promises to transfer a certain amount of resources to its creditors during future time periods. Without debt creation, the government could have secured the usage of resources currently only through taxation. Inflation of the currency as a means of financing public expenditure in this model becomes a form of taxation and should be analyzed as such.

The introduction of unemployment suggests that a different sort of operation must take place when the government borrows. Regardless of the manner in which the government secures the funds, the public expenditure for resources does not necessarily involve any transfer of real resources *from* current private employments. If the government purchases the services of unemployed resources, no real transfer need take place; no private person *need* give up any disposition of economic goods and services. In one sense, therefore, no "real" borrowing from the private economy need take place at all. In the extreme case in which the government exclusively purchases the services of previously unemployed resources, the real costs of such resources need not be other than zero. The public expenditure undertaken may involve zero real cost.

This situation which allows resources to be secured at zero real cost may be achieved, however, only if the government is an efficient purchaser. Since no private person gives up any current disposition over resources, and no real transfer takes place, the government need make no promise to private people to pay them real income in future periods. The actual private disposition over current resources need not be reduced. To provide the monetary means for its actual purchases of resource services, the government may create money quite readily. *The efficient means of purchasing the services of un-*

employed resources is through inflation of the currency. Individuals owning the resources concerned are made better off, and no one in the economy is made worse off.

In this currency inflation–public expenditure operation no public debt is created. Neither the present generation nor future generations undergo any sacrifice of utility or of real goods and services in order to secure the benefits accruing from the public projects constructed with previously unemployed resources.

Governments are not, however, always rational or efficient purchasers. Experience, especially that taken from the depression period of the 1930's, provides ample evidence that governments will refrain from creating money during depressions, and that they will, instead, create interest-bearing debt. And, even now, there is perhaps only a rather naïve hope that governments in the future would be any wiser and would improve substantially on this record.

If governments do choose deliberately to be inefficient purchasers, that is, if they sell interest-bearing securities instead of issuing noninterest-bearing money, no longer can the unemployed resources be put to work at a zero cost. *The zero real cost is a minimum which can only be reached by rational policy.* If interest-bearing debt is issued, some unnecessary real cost is introduced into the borrowing side of the fiscal operation, and even though the resources will otherwise be idle, the transference of these resources to the government must involve some future sacrifice of individual utilities.[1]

---

1. The oversight of this rather obvious point in the discussion of debt theory may be based on a slightly distorted meaning which is given to real cost in much careless textbook discussion. The opportunity or alternative cost of a good is often defined as those goods and services which could have been produced if the resources employed had been used in a different fashion. From this simple definition, the real cost of depression-built post offices, for example, has often been held to be zero, or nearly so, because the resources employed were not diverted from alternative employments, actually or potentially.

This line of reasoning overlooks the all-important point that the absence of alternative opportunities for resource employment sets a *minimum* of zero to the real cost of a good or service. There is nothing to insure that this minimum is always attained. It can be attained only with fully efficient purchasing. Individual analogies are easy to draw here. If I choose deliberately to pay a price for a good in excess of that set by the market forces, the real costs *to me* are in excess of the goods and services which the resources could have produced in alternative employments. The alternative or opportunity cost defined in the usual manner represents the *minimum* real cost, not the actual real cost.

If, in its sale of securities, the government withdraws funds from either consumption or investment spending, the subsequent utilization of these funds does nothing toward increasing the level of total employment. Debt creation under such circumstances is in all respects similar to the classical model already discussed. When debt creation during depression is discussed separately as a distinct fiscal operation, presumably the funds are drawn from idle balances and, therefore, when these are expended, idle resources are put to work. But if the securities sold are interest bearing, regardless of the amount or degree of unemployment existing in the economy, some real-debt burden is created. This debt burden is the real cost of putting the idle resources to work. And this real cost will be shifted forward to future taxpayers. If the government borrows to finance the building of a post office in a deep depression, the real cost of the post office is represented by the goods and services which taxpayers in the future could purchase if they were not obligated to finance the interest payments.

The interest-bearing, government securities are purchased by individuals and financial institutions from idle funds, and the real cost or primary debt burden is entirely unnecessary and could, and should, be avoided by direct money issue. At this point we may raise the question: Why is it necessary that the government pay interest on bonds sold to individuals or institutions who purchase these bonds from idle funds? What do these individuals or institutions give up in exchange for the claims to future incomes represented by the bonds? This question is answered when it is recognized that money as an asset yields some utility income to its holder in an uncertain world. Some sacrifice of current liquidity is involved in the exchange of idle cash for a government bond. The claim on future income may be considered a payment for this sacrifice of liquidity. But this payment is unnecessary, because the government does not add to its own liquidity in the process. It secures no additional liquidity from private people in the exchange. The government is always infinitely liquid so long as it possesses money-creating powers.

If the individuals and institutions do not purchase the bonds, they retain a more liquid cash position which, at least in their calculations made in the initial period, can be expected to yield them a utility income over future time periods. This alternative utility yield is comparable to the interest yield secured from the bonds. Bond purchasers are better off in future periods only insofar as these two expected yields differ.

The taxpayer, on the other hand, finds his utility in future periods reduced by the necessity of having to finance the interest payments. And it is reduced by the utility which he could have secured from the usage of the full amount of the transfer. The burden of debt, which is the real cost of the expenditure, rests on the future taxpayer just as in the classical model.

It seems clear that the sort of internal public debt discussed here is the model which many of the advocates of the new orthodoxy have used in constructing the debt theory which is currently espoused in our textbooks. Internal debt, considered as a substitute for money creation, rather than internal debt as a means for facilitating the real transfer of resources from the private to the public economy, is the model for the post-Keynesian construction. The failure of the new orthodoxy to see that its model of debt did not really overthrow the traditional theory lies in the confusion and the intermingling of the effects of securing the funds and the effects of spending them, the second methodological error mentioned. When unemployment does exist, the return to be expected from public expenditure which puts the unemployed resources to work is represented by the whole amount of the additional real income which these resources produce. On the payments side, the real costs which are present are unnecessary, and, if incurred at all, represent exchanges of claims on future income for current sacrifices of liquidity. Hence, the two sides of the fiscal operation embody quite different orders of magnitude, something which is not normally present in the classical model. In the latter, the debt-expenditure decision may be genuinely marginal; that is, the benefits and the real costs may be in roughly comparable dimensions. In the unemployment model, the benefits overwhelm the real costs in any absolute sense. This discrepancy explains the relative overemphasis on the benefits from debt-financed expenditure, but it does not remove from existence the real cost, and hence a real primary debt burden, albeit wholly an unnecessary one.

If the government is wise in such situations, it will issue currency outright. If it does this, the rate of return on its outlay will be infinite in real terms, or at least potentially so in the extreme case in which only unemployed resources are put to work, and no effects on prices take place. (This is the familiar assumption that there exist no bottlenecks in the economy to cause any price inflation until a full employment position is attained.) The cost of creating money is zero or nominal and the return is measured in the full amount of additional income generated. However, even if the government chooses to ignore this most efficient manner of financing expenditure during the depressions, and instead decides to issue interest-bearing debt as a means of securing idle cash from private hoards and from excess reserves of banks, the rate of return over its outlay is still likely to be tremendous.

This situation is not likely to be found often in the case of the private individual borrower, and, in this respect, public debt in depression is different from private debt. But the fundamental similarity is not modified since the private borrower could conceptually find himself in such a situation. The government in a depression is analogous to the individual who has secretly located a rich gold mine, and who needs only a shovel to begin work. The rate of return over the outlay on the shovel promises to be extremely high, and if the individual borrows to finance the purchase, he will certainly find himself far better off than had he remained idle. But this does not mean that he should consider the shovel to be free. To make the analogy more complete, however, we should have to allow the individual to have an old shovel around which he overlooks, one which would have done the job equally well. No borrowing is really required so his rate of return over cost could be infinite (labor cost neglected). It is not that the basic analogy between the public and the private economy becomes false during depression situations, but rather that the public economy is faced with a rare opportunity to make a tremendous return.

Similar conclusions may be reached in regard to the contrast made by the new orthodoxy between external and internal debt. When depression conditions prevail, the internal debt form is always indicated by purely market criteria. If fully rational the government will print money, that is, "borrow" at a zero rate of interest. If less than fully rational, it may choose to use internal debt as a substitute for money creation, paying a nominal return to reward people for the sacrifice of current liquidity. Assume, however, that liquidity preferences are extremely high, and that internal debt creation, even though the funds are to be drawn solely from private hoards, involves a high rate of interest, higher than the external borrowing rate. In this case the external rather than the internal loan is indicated, *provided that the same task can be accomplished with each.* The purpose of the borrowing must be that of securing funds which, when used, will bring idle resources into production.

This suggests that funds must be in units of domestic currency and that they must be expended in the domestic economy. In many cases, the external borrowing operation may not make this possible. In these, the rate on external relative to internal loans is not relevant. The internal loan exists as the only possible alternative to money creation. The external borrowing operation may necessarily be *real* in the sense that the borrowing economy secures the current usage of resources drawn from outside its geographical limits.

If, on the other hand, external borrowing allows a country to secure funds of domestic currency, or of an international currency convertible readily into domestic currency, the external loan will be the efficient form if the loan rate is lower than that required for the internal loan. Of course, it must be kept in mind that neither loan form is efficient when compared to money creation.

It may be concluded that the difference between the external and the internal loan is not relevant so long as they both apply to the same task. But if the one involves real borrowing of resources from abroad while the other implies merely the putting to work of previously unemployed resources, no comparison is possible. We are talking about two kinds of fiscal operation here, not about two kinds of loans.

From the above discussion it is not difficult to understand why and how the basic propositions of the new orthodoxy were developed. The difference in the alternatives faced by government during periods of deep depression and those normally faced by private people appeared to suggest a fundamental distinction between public and private debt, between internal and external debt, and between the possibility of shifting the burden in the one case and the other. As we have shown, these fundamental distinctions do not exist.

The basic confusion involves a comparison of public debt, as a form of or substitute for money creation, with private debt which is normally real in the sense that the borrowing operation does require the withdrawal of economic resources from current usage by some other economic units, within or without the economy.[2] It does not seem likely that this confusion would have de-

2. During periods of depression, the creation of private debt may also serve as a reasonably good substitute for money creation. Insofar as money borrowed to put resources

veloped if governments in the Great Depression had adopted rational monetary policy and created money in the direct manner. Instead they chose to sell securities internally to finance deficits, at low or nominal rates of interest. Some of these securities were drawn from the excess reserves of the banking system, some from private hoards. In either case, much of the depression-born debt was equivalent in effect to new money creation. But the operation appeared to be a debt operation, and was discussed as such, since debt instruments were transferred to private people, instruments which represented an obligation of the government to pay an interest when due.

The funds so raised did not, when used, cause the government necessarily to bid away resources from private employments. Some resources previously unemployed were put to work. Debt issue when coupled with such expenditure appeared always to be desirable, something which could not apparently be claimed for private debt. In this way, the whole new approach to the public debt was built up, an approach which is applicable only to the narrowest of irrelevant comparisons. The advocates of the new orthodoxy were really comparing the issue of public debt, *combined with the expenditure of the funds raised,* with the policy of no action on the part of government. In this comparison, the first alternative is clearly to be preferred during periods of deep depression. No resources are given up currently, and even though they must pay interest in the future, that is, bear the primary debt burden, taxpayers are still likely to be much better off as a result of the combined borrowing-expenditure operation.

On the other hand, when they considered private debt, the advocates of the new orthodoxy were thinking of a real borrowing operation in isolation from the expenditure. Only this can explain the idea that private debt is nec-

---

to work comes from hoards, no real transfer of resources takes place. Cf. Emerson P. Schmidt, "Private *versus* Public Debt," *American Economic Review,* XXXIII (March, 1943), 119–21.

When liquidity positions are considered, the issue of any debt, public or private, must serve as a partial substitute for money creation. That is to say, any debt, even if *real,* will introduce additional "moneyness" into the economy, at least to some degree. This is obvious when public debt is considered; it is less obvious for private debt. But, as McKean has shown, the illiquidity or "non-moneyness" of the debt obligation for the debtor cannot fully offset the liquidity or "moneyness" of the debt claim for the creditor. (See R. N. McKean, "Liquidity and a National Balance Sheet," *Journal of Political Economy,* LVII [1949], 506–22. Reprinted in *Readings in Monetary Theory* [New York, 1951], pp. 63–88.)

essarily burdensome, and that the carrying of private debt is oppressive. Had the expenditure side of the private debt been added into the picture, as it was with the public debt, the oppression would have been seen to arise only if the original combined borrowing-expenditure operation was unwise. A wisely chosen, debt-financed private undertaking may, similar to the public debt in deep depression, create much more income than it costs over future time periods. And, when compared with the no-debt alternative, the combined operation may actually be highly beneficial to the debtor. The new orthodoxy of the public debt and its central propositions were thus built up on the basis of an asymmetrical analysis of public and private debt. If we limit the comparison to the borrowing side, as this essay has done in preceding chapters, there is no distinction to be drawn. But if we include both the borrowing and the expenditure side, there is no distinction either. And the whole question of whether or not future generations of taxpayers in the public debt case and private debtors in the other are better or worse off depends on a comparison of the productivity of the project financed with its real cost.

10. War Borrowing

An overwhelming proportion of the outstanding public debts of all nations represents debt which was originally created to finance public expenditure during periods of war. It will be useful to examine this war-created debt as a special case.

The classical model which has already been thoroughly developed is fully applicable for that portion of war borrowing which represents a wholly *voluntary* transfer of economic resources from private to public uses. No additional discussion of this type of war debt is needed. Government sale of securities to individuals or to nonbanking institutions during the war periods is no different, in economic effect, from the sale of such securities during periods of substantially full employment. If, during the initial phases of a war, some unemployment exists, war borrowing might take on some elements of the Keynesian as well as the classical model. But no essentially new elements appear which warrant further discussion.

The classical model is clearly inappropriate for the portion of war borrowing which implements or facilitates the transfer of real resources from the private to the public economy *involuntarily*. Government sale of securities to the banking system introduces a unique operation which seems to combine elements of the classical and the unemployment models. Some further discussion of this sort of war debt is necessary.

Periods of deep depression are not the only ones in which government may employ public debt issue as a means of accomplishing the effects of direct currency creation. Government borrowing from the banking system during war periods is of this nature. If the government borrows from the system in such a way that the borrowing-expenditure process itself creates sufficient excess reserves to finance fully the banks' purchases of bonds, the results are substantially identical to an outright operation of the printing presses with the same subsequent expenditure of the funds.

A significant share of the outstanding national debt of the United States was created in this way during World War II. In December, 1939, the banking system held $18.4 billion in federal government securities. This total had increased to $115 billion by December, 1945. The increase was divided between the commercial or member banks and the Federal Reserve Banks in an approximately four-to-one ratio. By the process of borrowing one fourth of the additional $100 billion from the central banks, sufficient excess reserves were created (when the funds were spent) to allow the member banks to purchase the other three fourths. By this operation, the excess reserves of commercial banks were continually increased, and with these excess reserves they were able, and encouraged, to purchase government securities yielding a low, but positive, interest return. No liquidity was sacrificed in the operation, and, as Paul Samuelson once suggested, it could have been a 1 per cent war as easily as a 2 per cent one.[1] This manner of financing a large part of World War II expenditures was the major cause of the postwar difficulties in preventing and controlling inflation effectively.

The effects upon the general level of prices stemming from this type of debt creation are equivalent to the direct creation of currency. In this the operation is akin to depression-born debt which is financed out of private hoards and excess bank reserves. The only difference is that, in the latter case, individuals and financial institutions do sacrifice some liquidity in exchange for the claims on future income which is transferred to them in the form of debt instruments.

On the spending side, however, this war borrowing operation takes on classical overtones. When the funds secured in exchange for debt instruments are expended, resources are purchased which would have otherwise been used by private people. A real transfer of resources from the private to the public sector of the economy does take place. This transfer is, however, only superficially similar to that which takes place in the classical model. The wartime transfer is not effected by any reduction in private disposition over

1. Paul A. Samuelson, "The Effect of Interest Rate Increases on the Banking System," *American Economic Review*, XXXV (March, 1945), 16–27.

economic resources when the debt is issued. No private person suffers current sacrifice of goods and services until and unless the funds are spent. The borrowing side involves no part of the real transfer. This real transfer is wholly effected on the expenditure side by the incremental purchasing power which the newly acquired funds make available. The expenditure of the debt-financed funds creates inflation, and the inflation facilitates the real transfer. Thus, completely unlike the classical case in which bond purchasers voluntarily abstain from current usage of economic resources in exchange for future income claims, private people during the period of expenditure give up current command over resources involuntarily. With their given money incomes, individuals find that they are unable to purchase as many real goods and services as before the combined debt-expenditure operation takes place. These effects occur whether the inflation takes the open or the repressed form. If there is open inflation, individuals are confronted with higher prices. If the inflation is repressed by some sort of direct controls, they cannot freely purchase as many goods and services as they should like at established prices. In either case, they give up real goods and services which the government acquires. And there is no *quid pro quo* transaction involved here at all. Individuals give up current real income with no promise of future income. Inflation is equivalent to a tax which coercively imposes upon individuals some sacrifice of current resources.

This type of government borrowing, coupled with the subsequent expenditure of the funds, is important for our purposes because it allows us to locate other sources of support for the basic propositions of the new orthodoxy. Much of the interest in the theory of public debts, and consequently much of the discussion, has arisen from wartime borrowing. And here the failure to distinguish between the effects of the securing of the funds and the spending of them has been evident. The idea that the primary real burden of public debt must be borne by the generation living during the period of the initial borrowing operation seems to have stemmed from an implicit consideration of this particular model of war borrowing, to the exclusion of all other possible cases. If the two sides of the combined borrowing-expenditure operation are not separated, the primary real burden may, somewhat legitimately, appear to fall on the currently living and not on future generations.

But here the error is identical to that which is involved when depression-created debt is considered. If the borrowing alone is considered, a primary real burden is present which is shifted forward in time to the shoulders of future taxpayers. So long as the debt instruments carry with them some obligation to transfer to bondholders some future incomes, future taxpayers bear a real-debt burden. This is the cost side of the fiscal operation.

This burden of debt, or real cost of securing the funds, may be as low as desirable, since debt issue here is not a genuine "market" transaction. The burden will depend upon the amount of subsidy paid to the banking system. And this burden may be, and normally will be, dwarfed in significance by the *burden of inflation* which the debt operation facilitates. This burden of inflation must be borne largely by the generation living at the time that the resources are given up. It cannot be shifted easily. But this burden of inflation is not due to the debt *per se*. It arises solely from the fact that the government has not withdrawn, through taxation or through "real" borrowing, sufficient funds from the private economy to finance its purchases without a distortion of the general price structure. (This point was discussed briefly in Chapter 7.)

From all this it follows that the question "Who pays for the war?" is not equivalent to the question "Who bears the burden of the war debt?" The answer to the first question may be the one which the orthodox theory would suggest. If the war is financed largely by taxation and by inflation, whether the latter is directly implemented by currency creation or indirectly through the disguise of war borrowing from the banking system, individuals of the generation living during the war will pay most of the real cost. They will do so to the degree that *taxation* and *inflation* impose upon them, coercively, some current sacrifice of real goods and services. Inflation becomes a true tax, regardless of the way that it is financed, and the real burden of taxation does rest on the current generation.

Insofar as the inflation is made possible by the issue of debt, there is added to the current cost a supplemental real burden which is shifted forward to future generations of taxpayers. There is a burden of the debt in addition to a burden of tax (inflation). But this burden of debt may be insignificant in comparison to the larger burden of taxation (inflation).

But is there a "net" burden of debt in this model? Future taxpayers are, of course, worse off with the debt than they would be with its alternative, currency creation, which would have accomplished the same real purposes during the war period. We have stated that these future taxpayers bear the burden of war debt. But have we not overlooked the fact that this sort of war debt also involves beneficiaries who are better off with the debt? It is true that this sort of war borrowing, which provides a subsidy to the banking system, makes certain groups in society better off than they would be under currency inflation. Quite apart from the spending side of the operation, the issue of this type of debt benefits certain groups. No longer is debt issue a market transaction in which individuals or institutions exchange current command over resources or liquidity for future claims on income. The banking system essentially gets "something for nothing" in this operation. And the benefits from the debt accruing to individuals connected with the banking system may be offset against the real burden imposed on future taxpayers.

The recognition that, in this particular case in which debt issue does not represent a "market" transaction, beneficiaries of debt issue *per se* do exist does not modify the basic conclusions reached in the "general" theory of public debt developed in this book. First of all, the benefits which the banking system receives will tend to be fully capitalized at the moment of issue. Once this capitalization takes place, future receipts of debt interest cannot be classified as differentially beneficial to the holders of debt instruments. As we have argued earlier, future tax payments will not normally be fully discounted. Therefore, during any particular period subsequent to that of the initial debt issue, the social group, as a unit, will experience a "net" burden of debt.

Even if this capitalization aspect is neglected, however, the location of the burden of debt on future taxpayers is still legitimate. Let us assume that bondholders (commercial banks) do not capitalize future interest subsidies. (This assumption would amount to saying they do not carry government securities in their portfolios at capital values.) In future periods these institutions receive interest receipts equivalent to interest outpayments by taxpayers. These two items are offsetting in the aggregate, and no "net" burden could be defined. But surely here it is both appropriate and legitimate to separate the burden or cost of the debt issue from the benefits of the debt. There exists a beneficiary group, quite apart from any gains from exchange which may be present in the other cases. We have shown that the relevant alternative to debt issue here is currency creation which would accomplish the same real purposes. The question becomes that of determining the differential effects of debt issue. These effects may be separated into two parts: benefits and costs; and these two may be compared and evaluated. This is precisely equivalent to the procedure in the classical model.

One relevant alternative to debt issue is a failure to undertake the public expenditure. It is necessary to evaluate carefully the differential effects of the combined debt-expenditure operation. To do so we isolate the cost side, which is represented by taxes borne by future taxpayers, from the benefit side, which is represented by the social real income estimated to accrue to future citizens from the public project financed. Nothing in the classical model necessitates that there must be a "net" real burden when both sides are taken into account. In the classical model another alternative to debt issue is current taxation to finance the same expenditure. Here the differential effects of debt issue are taxes on future generations on the one hand and a lightened tax load on the current generation on the other. The social decision must always involve a comparison. To return to our example of war borrowing from the banking system, in which those who bear the cost may be from among the same generation as those who secure the benefits, it is necessary to separate the two sides of the account and to compare the costs with the advantages. Here the comparison will be based exclusively on distributional considerations. The debt is not necessary to finance the war; this can be accomplished through currency creation. The debt issue is justified here only if the distributional benefits more than offset the distributional costs. Note here that we cannot *a priori* make any such comparison as this. We cannot say that war borrowing from the banking system is socially undesirable. In the majority of cases, this sort of borrowing may lead to distributional effects which may be considered undesirable by many people. But nothing definite can be stated on this score.

There may, of course, be peacetime periods for which this war-borrowing model is applicable. For example, political pressures against higher interest rates during a period of prosperity and full employment may force the Treasury to refinance maturing long-term issues held by the public by the sale of new securities to the banking system, in part to the Federal Reserve Banks. In this case, the discussion of this chapter almost fully applies. The borrowing operation itself does nothing to reduce private purchasing power; and when the spending of the funds takes place (in this case retiring bonds held by the public) inflation must be the result.

Elements of this war-borrowing model may also be present in depressions. If the government borrows from the Federal Reserve Banks at a positive rate of interest, and subsequently from the newly created excess reserves of commercial banks, there is no sacrifice of liquidity in the purchase of the government securities. The minimum real cost of securing the fuller resource utilization remains zero, but the real burden of the debt must be offset here against the real benefits accruing to the interest-recipient beneficiaries.

The discussion of this and the preceding chapter reveals that much of the fuzziness of the new orthodoxy stems from a consideration of the depression borrowing from idle hoards and war borrowing from the banking system. As we have shown, neither of these forms involves "real" borrowing, that is, no reduction in private disposition over resources is required on the borrowing side of the fiscal operation. The transfer of resources in the depression case can be secured more efficiently through money creation since some resources are previously unemployed. In the war case, the transfer from the private to the public sector is facilitated solely by the incremental addition to purchasing power. This, too, could have been achieved by direct currency creation.

In either of these cases, if the debt alternative is adopted, some burden is imposed on future taxpayers. But this cost need not be large since bond purchasers only give up liquidity in the one case and nothing in the other. This cost of debt will tend to be insignificant when considered relative to the benefits from public expenditure in the depression case and relative to the burden of inflation in the war.

11. Public Debt and Inflation

In the two preceding chapters public debt issue which serves as a means of securing the effects of money creation has been discussed. Public borrowing in depression when there exist unemployed resources and public borrowing from the banking system in war provide the two separate cases. As suggested, neither of these forms of public debt is essential to accomplish the real purpose desired; the same results could be achieved by direct issue of currency without interest cost. Hence the real burden differentially associated with debt could be avoided. Debt issue in such situations becomes a rather clumsy way of inflating the currency.

Instead of serving as a substitute for money creation, debt issue should, fundamentally, be viewed as its opposite. The sale of government securities bearing positive interest returns is necessary only if some reduction in the purchasing power of private individuals and institutions is needed and if the process of sale accomplishes this reduction. The sale should involve some sacrifice of command over resources in the private sector. This suggests that public debt issue, in its real meaning, is appropriate only in two situations. The first is the genuinely classical case in which the government desires to replace the private demands upon resources with public or collective demands. The second situation is presented when stabilization criteria indicate that some reduction in private demand is needed quite apart from the public need for additional real resources. This occurs when inflation is threatened, and it is considered to be desirable social policy to prevent its taking place. It is with this second sort of debt issue that this chapter will be concerned.

Debt issue provides one means of combatting inflation since it involves an exchange of debt instruments for money. The sale of securities effectively withdraws money from the private sector, "destroys" currency in circulation.

As Henry Simons suggested:

> Borrowing is an anti-inflation measure, not a proper means for financ-
> ing reflationary spending. Borrowing is properly a means for curtailing
> purchasing power, private and governmental. To use it for injecting pur-
> chasing power is like burning the fire engines for heating purposes when
> there is an abundance of good fuel to be had free.[1]

Debt issue in inflationary periods has as its only purpose the reduction of
the liquidity in the private economy. It is not, therefore, akin to the classical
model in that government does not utilize the proceeds to purchase real goods
and services. Presumably, the government should neutralize the proceeds
collected from the sale of securities. (In the modern context this should mean
retiring that part of the national debt held by the central banks.) Only one
half of the classical debt-expenditure operation takes place, the opposite half
to that which takes place with war borrowing from the banking system. With
anti-inflation debt issue, government does withdraw current command over
resources from the private sector, but it does not use this source to finance
collective purchases. The result is deflation, at least in some relative sense;
deflation occurs when compared to what would happen were not the debt
issued. In the war borrowing case, which is the precise opposite, the result is
inflation.

Anti-inflation debt issue combined with effective neutralization of the
funds does not, of course, increase the government's employment of economic resources. Therefore, in the aggregate, private people living during the
period of debt creation retain disposition over the same quantity of real goods
and services with or without the fiscal operation. Debt creation acts so as to
modify the distribution of these currently produced real goods and services
among the separate classes of the population. For those who purchase securities, the exchange represents a voluntary sacrifice of current command over
real income in return for some greater command over real income in the future. This group possesses current purchasing power (money) which it could
employ if inflation (in a relative sense) were allowed to occur. This purchas-

---

1. Henry Simons, "On Debt Policy," *Journal of Political Economy*, LII (December, 1944).
Reprinted in *Economic Policy for a Free Society* (Chicago, 1948), p. 226.

ing power is exchanged for debt and, in this way, disappears. The interest receipts accruing to this group in periods subsequent to the initial one represent a part of an original *quid pro quo* transaction.

For the remaining groups in the economy, debt creation serves to improve their position. The purchasing power which they hold is not reduced in real value by so much as would be the case were debt not issued. The deflation (relative) imposed by debt creation must represent a net benefit to individuals who do not purchase the government securities. In the absence of debt creation, prospective security purchasers will utilize their power to purchase real goods and services causing prices to be higher than they would be in the alternative situation. And with prices higher, the purchasing power of the remaining groups in the economy is reduced.

The real cost of the operation rests on future taxpayers, as in all cases of pure-debt issue. If the purpose of debt creation is the prevention of inflation, that is, the maintenance of stability in the absolute price level, the cost of attaining this goal is shifted to future taxpayers. In a sense, this sort of fiscal operation can be conceived as a means through which portions of the population are "bribed" to refrain from exercising purchasing power through the promise of a larger share of future incomes. No coercion takes place in the process. As in the classical debt model previously discussed, only future taxpayers are *coerced* into giving up command over economic resources. Considered in the aggregate, and without regard to distributional considerations, future taxpayers will be worse off with the debt than they would be without it.

In the absence of the anti-inflationary debt creation, two alternatives are present. First, inflation could be allowed to occur, or, secondly, taxation could be levied to offset it. An example may be introduced for the first of these. Suppose that the current monetary-financial situation is such that a 10 per cent rise in prices will take place if no offsetting measures, either debt creation or taxation, are taken. Assume further that this increase will absorb the excess purchasing power which is present in the economy, and that once this price rise has occurred the economy will settle down again into some predictable stability pattern. It is possible to prevent this rise in prices by the issue of $5 billion of additional debt at a 4 per cent interest rate. The issue will create an annual interest charge of $200 million which must be borne by

future taxpayers. If debt is not issued, on the other hand, the generation living during the present period of the price rise will largely bear the inconven-
iences and the distributional burdens associated with the inflation itself. Individuals living in later periods will be burdened only insofar as the effects
are of permanent duration.

The remaining relevant alternative to debt issue for anti-inflationary purposes is current taxation sufficient to accomplish the same thing. Here the
differences are clear and simple. The cost of stability is exclusively placed on
current taxpayers in the one case; it is placed, at least in considerable part,
on future taxpayers in the other. The choice between the tax and the public
loan as a means of preventing inflation is only one aspect of the larger normative problem of "taxes versus loans." This problem will be discussed in its
general setting in the following chapter.

12. When Should
Government Borrow?

I. The Full Employment Model

It is sometimes good to clean house even if no guests are likely to call. This essay is conceived primarily as this sort of house cleaning. Its necessity at this late date represents, perhaps, a rather dismal commentary on the "dismal science." For the last quarter century ideas on public debts have been accepted which were effectively demolished in the nineteenth century. If this essay has contributed, even in a small way, toward a final clarification of public debt theory and toward the attainment of some ultimate consensus, it will have served its purpose. No implications for public policy need be present at all.

In fact, a considerable share of the recurring confusion may have stemmed from an overly close attention to policy at the expense of clear analysis. This statement is not made to deprecate the careful consideration of policy by economists; quite the opposite. Economic analysis was born in, and its important developments have all come from, a direct consideration of problems arising in the real world. Yet there is a vast difference between the consideration of real-world problems in the detached atmosphere surrounding the scholar and the many-tongued melee of the partisan political struggle. Political economy and not policy economics is the fountainhead of economic analysis. And political economy will produce useful normative propositions only to the extent that its analytical underpinnings are correct. The push and haul of the political process, on the other hand, leaves little room for careful analysis.

This book purports to have developed a "correct" analysis or theory of public debt. It has demonstrated the validity of three basic propositions which are diametrically opposed to those accepted currently by the great majority of economists. These "correct" propositions are:

1. The primary real burden of a public debt is shifted forward in time.
2. The analogy between individual or private and public debt holds good in most essential respects.
3. There is no important conceptual difference between internal and external debt.

In spite of the above statement that no implications for policy need be present, the application of this reversal of conception to those choice problems facing governmental agencies will allow some normative propositions to be constructed. Currently the most important of these choice problems is that given in the chapter title: When should government borrow? How will the debt analysis developed here help us in answering this important question? In this section I shall confine attention to the full employment or classical model. Later sections will extend the analysis.

WHEN SHOULD GOVERNMENT SPEND?

The question as to when the government should borrow cannot be answered apart from the fundamental normative question in fiscal theory: When should government spend? Or, differently phrased: How much should government spend? What proportion of the community's resources should be devoted to collective or public ends as opposed to private employments?

This brief and limited book on debt theory is not an appropriate place for an extended and conclusive discussion of the pure theory of public expenditure, even if this were possible. Some general consideration of this theory is, nevertheless, essential for our purposes. Clearly the government should borrow to finance a public expenditure project only if the expenditure itself should first be deemed "rational" or desirable for the community. The criteria for choosing between public and private expenditure, and among the separate types of public expenditure, cannot be neglected in debt theory.

I have argued elsewhere that there are essentially two approaches to fiscal theory.[1] In the first, the whole fiscal problem is discussed on the assumption

1. James M. Buchanan, "The Pure Theory of Government Finance: A Suggested Approach," *Journal of Political Economy*, LVII (December, 1949), 496–505.

that the community is an organic entity which possesses some unique and determinate value scale. In this case the fiscal problem reduces to one of simple maximization. The various public expenditures and the various tax items are so allocated or distributed as to maximize "social utility" in accordance with the scale postulated. Since this approach assumes or postulates the existence of some omniscient decision maker for the whole social group, fiscal theory becomes purely formal and amounts to nothing more than a definition of "efficiency" in the abstract sense. No problem arises concerning the possible differing effects of debt financing and tax financing. These two methods can exist as alternatives for the decision maker, and he (or it) can choose between them in accordance with ordinary maximization criteria. The discussion of Chapter 4 which demonstrated that debt financing does cause the real cost of public expenditure to be shifted to "future" generations is not relevant here. Real cost in terms of individual utilities sacrificed is not meaningful to the genuinely organic decision maker, and even if he chooses to take individual utilities into account, there is nothing to prevent his comparing present utilities with future utilities. The divergent time shapes of the tax and the debt payments present no problem.

This approach to fiscal theory may be criticized on the grounds that it is sterile and unproductive of useful results. It provides little that can be of guidance to the individuals actually participating in the process of collective decision making. The approach neglects the most important problem of all, that is, the manner in which collective decisions actually are made. In a society governed by some authoritarian and benevolent ruler, the organic approach might prove helpful. But societies of the Western world are not constructed in this way. Collective decisions are made through a complex and involved process of discussion, individual voting, representation in legislative assemblies, and, finally, some administrative discretion on the part of officials periodically elected or appointed. No individual anywhere in the decision-making chain can place himself in the role of the despot, and each individual will necessarily be limited in his information. Each individual will be selfishly interested in his own position *vis-à-vis* other members of the social group and also *vis-à-vis* other participants in the choice process.

In the approach to fiscal theory which recognizes the decision-making process, the manner in which alternatives are presented to the group becomes important in determining the sort of decisions which may be attained.

The fundamental choice remains that of determining the public and the private share of total economic resources. But the method of financing the public employment of resources becomes significant. The way in which the taxes are to be shared is relevant in determining whether or not the community will reach a favorable or an unfavorable decision regarding a particular public expenditure. Nothing is present in the structure to guarantee that the choices will be made at the appropriate "margins" as the organic theory might suggest. The differential effects on expenditure decisions resulting from the two broad financing alternatives, taxes and public loans, must be more carefully examined in this "individualistic" approach to fiscal theory.

In the new orthodoxy of public debt theory, taxes and public loans do not represent conceptually distinct alternatives at the most fundamental level of comparison. The real burden of public debt is alleged to be borne by individuals living at the time of the debt issue–public expenditure. The real cost of the public use of resources which is debt financed is met by the "current" generation, and is represented in the real goods and services transferred from private to public usage. This real cost is in its essential respects similar to that of public expenditure which is tax financed. Debt financing differs from tax financing only insofar as the distribution of the real cost of public expenditure among individuals of the *same* generation is different in the two cases.[2] From this it follows that a shift from the tax method of financing to the loan method or *vice versa* introduces no new problems of social choice. In each case, private citizens, through the procedural mechanism generally accepted for the reaching of collective decisions, attempt, however imperfectly, to answer the question "Are the resources more valuable in private or public employments?" The individual member of the community participates in this choosing process, at least ideally, and he casts his vote or exerts his influence in other ways on the basis of some subjective comparison of the individualized benefits which he expects to receive from the proposed public expenditure and the alternative benefits which he expects to receive from the retention of the share of the real cost which would fall his lot to bear.[3] Insofar as

2. "But the distribution of the real cost of a war in *time*—between past, present, and future—cannot be affected by the extent to which it is financed by taxation or borrowing. Borrowing affects rather its distribution among *persons*." (Henry C. Murphy, *The National Debt in War and Transition* [New York, 1950], p. 61.)

3. This is not to suggest that each individual will be purely selfish in making his deci-

the social or collective choice finally made reflects widespread participation by individuals and ultimate consensus, at least to the degree of reasonable acquiesence in the decision, there is little reason or use in attempting to measure in some objective manner the benefits from the public project. The subjective evaluation made by individuals in their roles as choosers provides a much superior guide to the "correctness" of the social decision. The task of the expert here becomes that of showing how the decision-making process itself may be improved, how information concerning alternatives can be increased, and how individuals can be presented with "fair" alternatives.

PUBLIC DEBT AND COLLECTIVE CHOICE

This essay has presented an alternative approach to public debt theory, one which does not accept the basic premises of the new orthodoxy. The vulgar approach re-established here destroys the relative simplicity with which decisions involving debt financing can be discussed. The similarity with tax financing disappears, and debt financing opens up a whole new set of problems in the realm of collective choice making.

The shifting of the primary real burden of public debts forward in time was shown to be possible in Chapter 4. Thus, the real cost of public expenditure which is debt financed must rest on individuals *other* than those who participate in the social decisions made at the time of the approval or rejection of any proposed expenditure. Individuals bear the costs in their capacities as *future* taxpayers, not in their capacities as individuals currently subjected to some coercive sacrifice of private enjoyments through the taxing mechanism. The fact that resources are physically shifted from private to public employments during the initial time period is unimportant when individual positions are analyzed.

This destroys the individual comparison of benefits from public expenditures and the costs of these expenditures which is possible in the case of taxes, and which would be possible with public debts if the new orthodoxy

sion. An individual may or may not include certain social values in his own value scale which is relevant for his participating in collective decisions. For example, an individual may consider it beneficial to him individually to provide aid for the poor people of Tongatabu even though he realizes that this expenditure of public funds can in no way affect his own individual position in society.

of debt theory were true. The purchase of government securities is an ordinary market transaction which is in no way akin to a tax payment. No individual or group of individuals suffers any "burden" or bears any "real cost" during the initial period of debt issue and public outlay, except insofar as the tax obligations for future periods may be capitalized.

The implication for individual rationality in the making of social decisions is obvious. If any individual benefits at all are expected to accrue currently from a proposed public expenditure, the individual when making his choice between the public debt–public expenditure and the no debt–no expenditure alternatives will always tend to favor the former over the latter. In such cases, the choice processes usually embodied in democratic institutions cannot be expected to provide correct decisions, upon any criterion of correctness. The individual chooser cannot fairly compare benefits and costs. This remains true even if the decision making assumes the ideal or town-meeting form. The fiscal illusion is magnified if the distribution of future taxes is not made clear at the time of debt issue.

Recognizing the built-in bias toward extended public expenditure which the possibility of debt issue introduces, some might be led to suggest that decisions of the nature which involve debt financing of short-term public projects are not suitable for widespread individual participation, that is, not suitable for democratic choices, and that, for such choices, the skilled administrator or the trained bureaucrat must be relied upon.

Such an argument might proceed as follows: Whereas the individual will tend to take primary or exclusive account of his own interests as a private citizen, the trained bureaucrat can think in terms of the over-all "social" interest. This interest can embody the welfare of future generations of taxpayers as well as current generations. The bureaucrat can thus reach reasonably objective decisions from a comparison of the "social" benefits to be gained from the public expenditures and the "social" costs which are involved in the tax payments necessary to service and to amortize the debt. In both the estimation of benefits and of costs, he will discount some future stream of payments or returns to arrive at some present values, and he will base his final decision on a comparison of these present values.

With this sort of reasoning we are thrown back into some organic or "social welfare function" approach to fiscal theory. Since it is impossible to construct an acceptable social value scale upon which such an individual could make decisions, this approach provides little aid in meeting the issue faced. Surely no one would seriously suggest allowing the bureaucrat to impose his own scale of values upon society as a whole.

A more acceptable, and more satisfying, implication of the analysis above is that the public loan should not be considered to be an appropriate financing method for short-term public expenditure projects. The process of social decision making in a modern democratic state is complex at its best, and this process should not be forced into positions where its very operation must produce biased decisions. In the "classical" model which assumes substantially full employment of economic resources, public debt issue should never be allowed to appear as an alternative method of financing public expenditures, the benefits of which are presumed to accrue, in whole or even in part, to individuals making the choices. The tax is the only appropriate financing medium for such expenditures.

As is true in so many cases, we find some protection along these lines already built into the fiscal conventions and traditions of the Western democracies. Public debt issue has normally been conceived as appropriate only for the financing of genuine public investment. This conception has been based upon the classical theory of public debt which this essay re-establishes. And early writers were clear in their perception that access to debt issue might lead to irresponsible spending decisions on the part of legislative assemblies and executives.

The limitations of debt financing to capital investment projects seems to have been based also upon an additional ethical premise which is perhaps less acceptable. The limitation stems, in part at least, from the heritage of the benefit principle of taxation, coupled with the classical views on the location of debt burden. Insofar as public expenditures benefit current generations, the benefit principle suggests that they should be financed wholly from tax revenues. But if public expenditures are anticipated to yield income in future time periods, future generations will receive the bulk of the benefits. Therefore, some portion of the real costs should be placed on future taxpayers; this is accomplished through the financing of the expenditure by debt rather than taxation. Despite the apparent attractiveness of this argument when first considered, it has no real basis. The benefit principle for the distribution of the tax burden among individuals and groups of a single generation has long since been discarded, and it is now almost universally accepted that the "fisc" must act to redistribute real income among individuals, intentionally or unintentionally. If this is possible for individuals in a single generation, the fisc can equally well redistribute real incomes among individuals living in separate generations. There is no fully acceptable ethical reason why the government should not impose real costs upon future taxpayers through the financing of current public expenditure through bond issue, just as there is no ethical reason why government should not provide real net benefits for future taxpayers by financing capital projects out of current tax revenues.

The limitation of debt financing to genuinely long-term projects must be based upon the effects on the choice process. But these results must be applied positively as well as negatively. If democratic decision making will not produce correct results when debt financing is made available for short-term public expenditure projects, the same must apply to tax financing when this is offered as the means for financing genuinely long-term projects. Individuals will, in this case, take account of the real cost of the expenditure which will be borne, primarily or exclusively, in the present. They will be forced to undergo genuine sacrifice of current enjoyments in order to meet the tax increases necessary to finance the proposed project. On the other hand, they will not estimate the future benefits of the project properly. Some capitalization of future benefits will, of course, take place, just as some future tax capitalization will take place in the converse situation, but, by and large, individuals will underestimate both future benefits and future tax payments when they are called upon to make social decisions.

This point perhaps requires some further explanation and clarification. In saying that private people discount future taxes and future benefits too heavily in the making of social or collective decisions, are we not supporting the argument that all private decisions which concern the utilization of capital assets will be irrational, and that the basic decision of individuals regarding the rate of capital formation will be biased in the direction of too much current consumption relative to savings? The answer to this question is *no*. I shall argue here that there is an *additional* element in the making of collective decisions which prevents the individual from making a proper comparison of present and future values even though this same individual can make rational choices between present and future values in his private decisions.

The Ricardian argument that taxes and loans exert identical effects on the economy was introduced and briefly discussed in Chapter 4. This argument was based on a direct analogy with the individual taxpayer who should be indifferent between paying a current tax of $2,000 and an annual tax of $100, provided only that the rate of interest is 5 per cent. The extraordinary tax and the public loan were thus held to be identical. This argument assumes, of course, that the individual taxpayer fully discounts the future obligations which he and his heirs must meet. Therefore, through this capitalization process, the taxpayer-voter, at the time of decision, bears the real cost of the debt-financed public expenditure just as he does the real cost of the alternative tax-financed expenditure. The limited time horizon of the individual human being presumably has no effect on the individual behavior in choosing between the tax and the loan forms.

It is quite clear that the Ricardian argument would be acceptable if individuals lived eternal lives, or if family relations were so close that fathers considered their sons as parts of themselves for estate planning purposes. The latter relation holds good to a certain extent, of course, although perhaps not so much as in Ricardo's time. But a more realistic approach to the problem would be one in which individuals are recognized as individuals. And although man's life is not quite so nasty and brutish as it was for Hobbes, it remains short. The individual must operate within a reasonably limited time horizon. If this is accepted, the Ricardian argument falls, and the tendency will be for future payments and returns in future periods to be too heavily discounted *in collective decisions,* although this will have *no effect on private decisions.*

In order to contrast the individual's behavior in a private decision with a public one, let us introduce a simple, although scarcely obvious, example of a private decision involving some calculation of a future stream of returns. We shall assume that the individual is fully rational in that he attempts in all cases to maximize some present value of expected utility over time. Let us assume now that the individual owns a tract of growing timber. We shall further assume that this individual has no interest whatsoever in posterity, and that he knows that he will die in five years. His time horizon is effectively limited to the five-year period. What is there to insure that he will, in fact, act in accordance with the criterion of maximizing the value of this asset? Will not the limitation of his life span cause him to undertake cutting practices which will be contrary to the interests of the whole social group?

A reasonably thorough understanding of the price mechanism will indicate that the limitation of the individual's time horizon will not, in any way, affect his behavior in tending his capital asset. Regardless of the programmed consumption of income over the five-year period, he can still maximize this income stream by maximizing the present value of his capital asset at every point in time. And if the asset maintains a higher present value standing as growing timber than as sawn wood, he will maintain it as timber. He will, therefore, be following the dictates of the social group in evaluating the timber. If this social evaluation indicates that the present value of the tract is maximized by continually growing timber, the individual owner can maximize his five-year income stream by either of two processes. He can sell off portions of the tract at the increasing capital value, or he can borrow against the increased value of the whole tract. He will be acting foolishly if he cuts the timber under these conditions. This behavior pattern depends, however, upon the existence of a *market* for the capital asset at any one point in time, or on a source of funds which may be borrowed with the capital asset as collateral.

It is the absence of these marketability conditions which renders the individual's decision on public choices different from his private decisions. In social or collective decisions the time shape of the expected income stream is important, since the individual cannot always effectively translate these into present values. If the owner of the timberland could not sell off the increasing value asset or borrow against it, the limitation upon his life span would tend to encourage him to disregard the present value criterion, that is, social evaluation, and to undertake socially undesirable cutting practices. The increasing capital value is desirable to the individual under consideration here only because it may be converted at any point in time into income. If this outlet is not available to him, the increase in capital value which is brought about by continuous abstention from usage will not weigh so heavily in his decision making. He will discount the future more heavily than the social interest would dictate.

The individual in participating in social or collective decisions is analogous to the individual who does not possess the available market for his capital asset. He will, therefore, tend to discount the future somewhat too heavily, even though he remains fully rational individually in so doing. Let us consider the case of the individual who, as a voter, is choosing between a quasi-permanent asset, say a school building, and a less permanent employment of funds, say a county fair. Let us further assume that, if some omniscient calculating machine were present which could effectively "read" individual evaluations through all future time, the present values of these two assets would be equivalent. If this were the case, the individual would choose the expenditure on the county fair rather than the school building. This is because, once he commits his individualized share of funds for school construction, these funds are committed once and for all. There is no market recourse which will allow him, upon retirement, death, or migration, to sell off his individualized share in the school building at some current capital value. Nor can he use such an individualized share of a collectively owned asset as collateral for borrowing purposes. The asset can be expected to yield up "income" over future time periods, but the individual can realize the enjoyment of such income only if he happens to be living during such time periods. The possibility of his changing the shape of his income stream through a conversion of one part of this into a capital value is closed for publicly owned assets. Therefore, the individual's interest in public assets will depend strictly upon his time horizon within which his decisions are made. There is no built-in mechanism which makes him adjust his time preferences to a market rate of discount similar to that which exists for the sphere of private decisions.

The above analysis indicates that an individual with a limited time horizon will tend to undervalue future benefits from public investment projects. The absence of a market for the assets affects his behavior in choosing. It is perhaps not evident that the same absence of a *market* will cause the individual also to undervalue (in a relative sense) future tax payments which are necessary to service debt which has financed current capital outlay. If an individual tries to borrow privately, he can do so only if he provides sufficient collateral. The existence of assets (his own or those of his friends or relatives) against which his private debt obligations are put insures that this individual will effectively pay the full borrowing rate set by market forces, regardless of the time horizon. If this were not true, the individual in our example with a time horizon of five years and absolutely no interest in posterity would maximize his satisfaction by borrowing as much as possible and not paying the money back at all. But without collateral the individual cannot enter the loan market.

The case is different with public debt, and the effect of public debt issue is that it allows such individuals to "borrow" without effectively paying the debt off during their life span. If his time horizon is effectively limited to five years, the individual, in trying to choose between the issue of public debt to finance a public expenditure and taxation to finance the expenditure, will clearly be biased toward debt. He will capitalize his tax payments only for the five-year period. And this may represent only a portion of the real costs of the project. The individualized rate of return on short-term investment projects which are debt financed may be very great. Therefore, just as in the opposite case, the future is discounted too heavily insofar as collective decisions are concerned.

This analysis of the collective decision-making process is useful in yielding negative conclusions. It indicates that democratic institutions will probably not be able to decide properly if public debt issue is made possible for genuinely short-term public projects, and that similar results follow when tax financing is applied to genuinely long-term projects. This provides, however, only a partial answer to the question posed in the chapter title: When should government borrow? Quite clearly, it should borrow only to finance long-term or capital investment projects which are expected to yield benefits over future time periods. But the analysis so far has not examined this particular choice explicitly.

We shall now assume that a public expenditure is proposed which is to be devoted to the construction of a public project which is not expected to yield benefits until future periods and that these benefits are expected to extend over many periods. A dam might be a good example here. Private people, in their capacities as choosers, will tend to discount too heavily both the future benefits and the future costs which are involved. Both sides will enter into the individual's behavior pattern in distorted form. This suggests that decisions made about long-term projects are likely to be somewhat more erratic than are decisions which introduce the tax financing of short-term projects. The best that can be expected in regard to a decision of this nature is that the errors made on the two sides are roughly offsetting in their effects on individual behavior. There is, however, and this should be emphasized, absolutely no assurance that they will be offsetting. In a very real sense, individuals choosing between a long-term project to be financed by a public loan and no project, are placed in the position of third parties. They are trying to assess the costs to future taxpayers and weigh these against the benefits to future taxpayers and arrive at some decision. To be sure, there is some capitalization on both sides of the account, and individuals consider their own future interests carefully in making any decision as well as those of their heirs. But to a considerable degree, at any rate, they must be acting as third parties. The subjective evaluation which compares the individualized benefits with the real costs in the tax-expenditure decision is missing.

In spite of these inherent deficiencies in decision making, long-term public projects do present themselves and their financing cannot be ignored. The best that can be done is to insure that, insofar as individuals try to estimate accurately the future benefits in comparison with future costs, as much information as possible concerning the extent of these future income and payments streams be provided. It becomes essential that some method of financing the debt service and amortization be adopted *at the time of the initial decision.* It is the height of folly to allow individuals to choose a bond issue to finance a long-term project with no corresponding means of paying the service charges. A future tax obligation can be impressed upon the individual behavior pattern only if it is institutionalized in a specific tax schedule. To be sure, these future taxes will be discounted too heavily (as will the benefits), but the only chance for these two sides to be roughly offsetting lies in the earmarking of some revenue source for debt service at the time in which debt is created. It was the recognition of this point that led Wicksell to stress the especial importance of simultaneous decision on spending and future taxation in the case of government loans.[4]

The principle of simultaneous decision on public debt creation and the levy of taxes sufficient to service and amortize the debt is in opposition to the principle of nonearmarking of funds which is to be found in much of modern budgetary theory and practice. This represents yet another portion of fiscal orthodoxy which requires considerable re-examination, but this essay is not the place to undertake this task. But, in relation to the question under consideration, the earmarking of funds to finance the servicing of the debt is a necessary condition for any sort of approach to individual rationality in the choosing process.

Another aspect of the conservative fiscal tradition which is sometimes encountered is that public debt should be issued to finance self-liquidating projects, meaning by this projects which will directly yield to the government

4. Knut Wicksell, *Finanztheoretische Untersuchungen* (Jena, 1896), Chap. 6.

a money return sufficient to service and to amortize the debt. The principle upon which this idea is based is the same as that discussed above. If a project is self-liquidating, then sufficient revenues are automatically earmarked for debt service from the start. For public projects of this sort, which must be of a quasi-private nature such that services may be marketed to individuals directly, debt financing is certainly appropriate. Many examples come to mind here. Perhaps the most familiar are municipal electric power facilities, municipal water and sewage systems, toll highways, and other projects of like nature.

It seems evident, however, that the limitation of public debt financing to self-liquidating projects would be overly restrictive. Despite the fact that the services produced by a project may not be privately marketable (due to the inherent indivisibility of many public services), if the project is genuinely of the capital investment sort, public debt financing seems appropriate if any approach to some rational allocation of public funds between projects yielding primarily current services ("consumption" projects) and those yielding services in the future is to be expected. Once this is admitted, however, the question is immediately raised concerning the appropriate distinction between the "consumption" type of public expenditure and the "investment" type. How is the principle developed here to be applied in practice?

The first criterion which is sometimes encountered is the physical characteristics of the project financed. Public debt issue is sometimes defended if the project takes on a measurable physical form, that is, if it takes up space. But surely this is not useful as may be shown by the example of educational expenditure. The issue of public debt to finance a school building because it is a physical construction is no more appropriate than the issue of debt to finance an increase in teacher salaries. Both these are "investment" projects in a very real sense, and the returns to the community can only be expected to be produced over a long succession of time periods. This example suggests, however, that most public expenditure of funds can, in a sense, be classified as long term and that debt issue provides the appropriate means of financing.

Some limitation is provided at this point by another part of the traditional conception of the public finances. Public debt issue has been held to be applicable only to genuinely abnormal or extraordinary expenditure. In the abstract, this limitation cannot be defended, but it does provide a useful helpmate in practical fiscal policy. Let us refer to the school example.

Presumably, the construction of the school building is an abnormal expenditure, one which will not recur repeatedly over the several years of the future. On the other hand, teacher salaries must be paid each year; this represents a recurring expenditure. Fiscal prudence would seem to suggest that borrowing is inappropriate for the latter type of expenditure but suitable for the former. Current taxation sufficient to finance recurring expenditure, even of the "investment" sort, seems to be dictated in lieu of repeated issues of debt. Recurring expenditures of this nature could be capitalized and financed by one large initial issue of debt. This procedure seems hardly practicable, however, given the proclivity of governments to spend all currently available funds. Over a long time period, financing recurring expenditures from current taxation and from debt would produce equivalent results in any one time period, provided only that the same amount of total expenditure is undertaken. The rate of current taxation would be the same in either case whether the funds are applied directly to finance new capital investment or to service debt for previously made investments. As we have repeatedly emphasized, however, the proviso is important here, since the two methods might have differing effects on the choice process. And here it seems clear that the requirement that current taxation finance directly all recurring capital expenditure will result in less of such expenditure over time than would be the case if such expenditure were to be debt financed, even with the requirement that future taxes must be earmarked for debt service at the time of issue.

The hypothesis which this analysis suggests is that, within the framework of currently accepted fiscal traditions and practices, long-term capital investment projects which assume physical forms and which are nonrecurring are over-extended relative to other public investment projects which are recurring and which do not assume physical forms. We see manifestations of this in the extreme emphasis on school building relative to the quality of instruction, on hospitals relative to the quality of service, and in similar examples.

Conclusions

The title of this chapter is "When Should Government Borrow?" And, in this first part, the full employment setting has been assumed. It was first suggested that the question could not be answered apart from the more fundamental question of fiscal theory: When should government spend? This basic question was briefly discussed, and it was shown that, in the context of democratic decision-making institutions, the answer depended upon the alternatives which were presented to individuals. These include the methods of financing, and debt financing, which does shift the real cost of expenditure to future generations, was shown to be wholly inappropriate for short-term or "consumption" public projects. Conversely, the exclusive reliance on tax financing was shown to provide decisions biased against long-term public investment projects. Here the issue of public debt was suggested, but the difficulties of decision making are not removed. Individuals, in choosing to finance a long-term public project by debt issue, were considered as third parties since these individuals, as choosers, neither will receive the benefits or bear the real costs. In order to produce any semblance of rational choice here, it was suggested that the levy of taxes sufficient to service and to amortize the debt and the earmarking of these tax revenues for this purpose are essential. And these steps must be taken simultaneously with the debt issue.[5]

5. It is evident that much of this discussion has direct relevance for the problem of *capital budgeting* which has been discussed during recent years. It has been proposed, by Beardsley Ruml and others, that public expenditures for current expenses be budgeted separately from public expenditures for capital outlay. Current tax revenues should, in this argument, be sufficient to cover only current expenses including debt service and amortization. The expenditures for capital outlay are said to be appropriately covered from funds raised by the sale of government securities, that is, by government borrowing. The liability which is represented by the new issue of debt is matched by the asset embodied in the capital investment.

This variation on the balanced-budget rule in the classical model of full employment is based largely on an analogy drawn from business financing. The analysis of the individual behavior in the collective choice process indicates that there is some merit in the capital budgeting approach. It shows that debt financing for long-term projects is desirable even in the full employment model. The individual's tendency to discount too heavily future benefits would cause long-term projects to be undervalued if tax financing alone were to be relied upon.

Capital budgeting as it is usually presented, however, does not include the specific earmarking of tax revenues for debt service and amortization which the analysis has indicated to be essential for reasonable rationality in the choosing process. It is necessary that the choosing individuals, whether voters, representatives, or administrators, be faced with both a future stream of benefits and a future stream of costs when decisions are to be made. And the vague knowledge that all debts must be serviced in the future is not sufficient protection here. A more fruitful approach would be that of separating from the regular budget entirely those projects to be debt financed along with the revenue sources assigned to them. In this manner, even though the projects are not self-liquidating in the

The limitation of debt issue to self-liquidating public projects was suggested as overly restrictive, and the limitation to extraordinary or abnormal investment expenditure, while useful in practice, was estimated to bias public decisions against the normal or recurrent public investment outlay.

My attempts to answer the question have been based upon a careful consideration of the democratic choice-making process. Primarily, the analysis has centered upon the behavior of the individual in trying to make his private decision as a voter, representative, or public choice maker in whatever capacity. In this decision I have assumed that the individual is rational and that he will make some attempt to weigh benefits against costs. But perhaps most importantly, I have assumed that there exists some general consensus upon the means by which social decisions are produced, if not upon each decision itself. In other words, my analysis is applicable to majority voting as a means of making social decisions if, and only if, the general consensus of the whole social group is that majority voting is the appropriate means of making decisions. This suggests that deliberate interclass or intergroup opposition is absent, and that deliberate redistribution among social classes through the fiscal system is present only insofar as the whole society acquiesces in such redistribution.

If these conditions are absent, the analysis will not hold. If, for example, the temporary current majority is controlled by the poorer classes who are determined to utilize the fiscal system in all possible ways to benefit their own group at the expense of the richer classes, and without their general agreement, the conclusions reached about decisions must be drastically modified. Unless individual decision makers can appropriately weigh real costs against real benefits in some meaningful fashion, the whole fiscal process takes on the appearance of purely partisan struggle, and any analysis which seeks to provide normative results is hopelessly doomed from the outset.

II. Nonclassical Models

When should government borrow? The analysis of Chapters 9 and 10 suggests the answer to this question in the nonclassical situations of depression

---

ordinary or commercial sense, the earmarked revenues serve to make them self-liquidating insofar as the social choice process is affected.

and war. Insofar as war borrowing represents real borrowing, that is, a voluntary transfer of real resources *from* the private to the public sector, the situation is the classical one and nothing need be added to the preceding discussion. The type of war borrowing especially noted in Chapter 10, however, consists in the sale of government securities to the banking system. This type of war borrowing, along with depression borrowing, was shown to be disguised currency creation. No real transfer of resources *away from* private usage is effected by the debt issue in such cases, and the interest payments associated with such issues are almost wholly unnecessary. The conclusion is, therefore, clear. The government should not issue nominal debt in either of these situations except insofar as it desires to utilize public debt issue as one part of a redistribution process. In depression situations, the same real purposes can be accomplished by the issue of currency bearing no interest. In war situations, the same real purposes can also be accomplished by currency issue, and direct issue in this case will serve the complementary purpose of making people more willing either to support taxation or to purchase real-debt instruments.

The question is not so easily answered in regard to anti-inflation debt which was discussed in Chapter 11. Here the sale of securities does act to reduce the purchasing power of individuals and, therefore, to fulfill a real function. But the alternative in this case is current taxation, and the analysis of "taxes versus loans" presented in Part I of this Chapter almost fully applies. The decision-making processes embodied in democratic institutions will be biased in favor of the debt-creation alternative. Since this sort of stabilization policy effectively shifts the burden onto future generations, it will be more strongly supported than current taxation. The argument suggests that, if only these two alternatives are considered, current taxation (fiscal policy) is a more desirable means of preventing inflation than debt creation, including the transformation of existing debt instruments so as to increase pure debt and decrease "moneyness" (monetary policy).[6]

The postwar experience is not conclusive, but it does suggest that democratic governments will rarely impose taxation explicitly to prevent the taxation which is implicit in inflation. The benefits to be secured from over-all

---

6. For a further elaboration of the distinction between "pure" debt and "monetized" debt, see the Appendix.

economic stability do not seem to motivate individual behavior sufficiently to make fiscal policy a fully effective anti-inflation weapon. If this is accepted, we must then compare real-debt creation with inflation itself. There can be little doubt but that the burden is differently distributed over time in the two cases. The burden placed upon future taxpayers by debt creation must be compared with the distributional evils of inflation itself, along with the taxation on the holders of cash balances which inflation represents. The conclusion may well be that of Henry Simons: "If we will not pay taxes to stop inflation, we must at least pay interest."[7] The danger of this lies, however, in the fact that the alternative of paying interest as a means of securing "voluntary" stabilization tends to cause the paying of taxes to be too much neglected.

7. Henry Simons, "On Debt Policy," *Journal of Political Economy,* LII (December, 1944). Reprinted in *Economic Policy for a Free Society* (Chicago, 1948), p. 222.

13. Should Public Debt Be Retired?

As of July, 1957, the federal government debt of the United States amounted to $272.5 billion. State and local units of government owe an additional $55 billion (estimated). The annual cost of servicing the national debt for fiscal 1958 is estimated to be $7.8 billion; state and local debt service charges will require perhaps an additional $1.7 billion.

These are significant totals even in the most prosperous economy that the world has ever known. Public debt cannot be relegated to the position of an unimportant or minor aspect of the nation's fiscal structure. And even should the question discussed in the last chapter never arise, the manifold problems arising from managing the existing public debt are continuous and difficult.

This book will not include a specific discussion of debt management. The management of the national debt introduces issues and questions of complexity and detail which are not essential to the main argument of this book.[1] For my purposes it will be useful to consider only those broader aspects of debt management which appear to be modified in some way by the reversal of conceptual approach.

The central issue in debt management concerns the rate at which public debt is to be retired. Should an active and vigorous attempt be made to reduce the interest-bearing public debt? There are several parts to this question, and each must be considered separately.

First of all, it is necessary to distinguish debt retirement as such from the means of financing such retirement. There are two ways in which net debt retirement may be financed, taxation and money creation. Only the first of

1. For a current attempt to construct an economic theory of debt management see Earl Rolph, "Principles of Debt Management," *American Economic Review*, XLVII (June, 1957), 302–20. For a general discussion of debt management in the immediate postwar period, see Charles C. Abbott, *Management of the Federal Debt* (New York, 1946).

these is open to subordinate units of government. Both are open to the central government which possesses money-creating powers. In the full employment model, however, money creation has effects which are equivalent to taxation. This makes it useful to consider this model separately. In this chapter I shall assume that the economy is characterized by full employment and a stable price level. Only in the following chapter shall I introduce the stabilization aspects of debt retirement operations.

Public debt instruments take several forms. Therefore, it is also necessary to specify what part of the debt is to be retired. The retirement of debt held by the commercial banks and the central banks has different effects from the retirement of debt held by individuals or by nonbanking institutions. In this chapter I shall consider only the retirement of public debt held by these latter groups. The retirement of bank-held debt cannot be discussed apart from the stabilization aspects; these will be fully explored in the following chapter. I shall assume here that the question is one of retiring debt held by individuals, the retirement to be financed by taxation.

This is not to suggest that the tax-financed retirement of privately held debt will be without effects upon the level of absolute prices or upon employment. The deflationary effect of the taxation must be compared with the inflationary effect of the repayment. The combined operation may be inflationary or deflationary in net terms, the result being dependent upon the relative propensities of taxpayers and bondholders to spend out of ordinary income, and the degree to which debt repayment does not represent an ordinary income payment for bondholders. Assuming roughly equivalent behavior patterns for taxpayers and bondholders, the combined operation is probably deflationary due to the fact that debt instruments possess some "moneyness." But there is no *a priori* way in which this effect can be established. It seems best, therefore, that this sort of taxation-retirement operation be examined for effects other than those upon the absolute price level.

We may first review briefly the implications for this question to be drawn from the currently orthodox theory. This theory makes a rather sharp conceptual distinction between the federal debt and the state and local debt. The federal debt is an internal debt, while state and local debts are external to the borrowing jurisdiction in large part. For the latter, the new orthodoxy would suggest a reasonably rapid rate of repayment in order to reduce the annual interest drainage out of domestic tax revenues. For the federal government debt, on the other hand, the new orthodoxy would suggest that the rate of retirement is not very important. This debt, being internal, involves a mere transfer of purchasing power from the taxpayers to the bondholders. While some secondary burden of the interest transfer is acknowledged, this is conceded to be relatively minor.

The approach of this book views debt retirement in a different light. It has been demonstrated that there is really little difference between internal and external debt. The fact that interest payments on public debt represent transfers of purchasing power from taxpayers to bondholders becomes more important. The sacrifice imposed on the taxpayer is a very real cost which is measured in terms of the alternative goods and services which he could otherwise enjoy were the debt service eliminated.

The implication of this approach is *not* that debt retirement must be attempted during all normal periods of economic activity. In the full employment model which we are considering, the alternatives to an active policy of debt retirement are tax reduction and public expenditure expansion. In reaching a collective decision, an attempt must be made to compare the benefits to be secured from each of these three alternatives. The benefits from current retirement of public debt will be enjoyed in large part by future taxpayers. They will be relieved of the necessity of having to finance the required interest transfers. On the other hand, the benefits from a reduced rate of current taxation (or a differentially lower rate) or from an expansion of current public expenditure of the "consumption" variety will be enjoyed primarily by those individuals living at the time in which the retirement decision must be made. If a society faced with an outstanding public debt makes a decision to undertake substantial retirement, it is deliberately providing future benefits at the expense of current enjoyments. From the analysis of the collective decision-making process which was briefly developed in the preceding chapter it may be readily inferred that decisions are likely to be biased against retirement. Experience in democratic countries seems to bear this out. Rarely have nations deliberately retired significant portions of their debts. In effect, a public debt, once created, will tend to be permanent unless some repayment mechanism is built into the original decision and this commitment is honored. The necessity for this built-in device for repayment seems to have been vaguely recognized by those early advocates for the establishment of sinking funds, although they became somewhat overenthusiastic over the effects of compound interest.

But at this point we are interested in the normative question "Should debt be repaid?" Whether or not the people acting collectively will choose to repay need not delay us here.

There are essentially three separate arguments which may be employed. Two of these will be found to lend support to a policy which considers the debt permanent and attempts no significant retirement. The third argument strongly suggests that an active policy of debt retirement should be attempted.

The Equity Argument

The first argument is a highly tenuous one in that it introduces again the whole question of equity as among separate generations of taxpayers. As we have indicated earlier, the benefit principle of taxation is no more applicable for allocating the costs of public expenditure among separate generations than it is for allocating costs among separate individuals or groups within a single time span. In a purely negative sort of way, however, this principle may be useful. The taxpayers living in 1958, for example, would be required to give up a substantial sum if the national debt were to be liquidated, once-and-for-all, during this calendar year. The argument that such liquidation should take place does not seem acceptable on any grounds. A part of the federal debt, even in a pure or nonmonetized sense, was created to finance World War II. Although this was perhaps a highly "productive" expenditure of funds, the incremental real income stemming from "victory" may be said to be permanent. The "benefits" from this war expenditure have become a part of the national capital. The 1958 taxpayer receives no greater share of this benefit than will the 1975 or the 2000 taxpayer. And neither had any voice in choosing debt creation over wartime taxation. It does not seem unreasonable to suggest on equity grounds, which should command wide acceptance, that the portion of the "pure" national debt created during war periods should be considered permanent and that no real effort should be made to retire it.[2]

2. As indicated in Chapter 10, a large part of nominal debt issued during World War II was not "pure" debt at all, but instead was disguised currency creation. Insofar as this

A similar conclusion may be reached with regard to that portion of real debt which was created for purposes which involve no directly measurable public investment. Debt issue which was used to finance purely wasteful expenditure must fall in this category, as must debt which was issued unnecessarily due to the failure of government to secure funds efficiently through money creation. This, combined with the war debt considered above, makes up a good part of the national debt, and this argument indicates that no serious effort should be made toward retirement. The refunding of this type debt into consols bearing no fixed maturity date would seem a reasonable management decision.

An extension of this argument may be applied to public debts which are created to finance specific capital improvement projects having a limited life. Only a small portion of the federal debt falls under this heading, but the greatest part of state and local debt fits in this category. Debts created to finance such projects as highways, parks, schools, and river basin developments are a few of the many examples which may be mentioned. The effective life of any specific investment project is limited, that is, the project will yield real income only over a finite period of time. The equity argument would suggest that the practices followed by private business firms be adopted for public debt of this nature. Debt should be fully amortized within the period of the effective life of the capital asset. Especially as applied to state and local units of government, this argument has additional merit in that such practice tends to preserve the credit rating of the borrowing unit. Debt retirement policy cannot be divorced from the effects on the securities market, although, for the national government, the connection may be quite remote.

Diminishing Marginal Utility

The second argument that may be used in support of a no-retirement policy represents an application of the conception which provides the theoretical support for progressive taxation. The whole basis of the argument is very shaky, and the more sophisticated students of public finance have long since discarded it, but it is still found in many modern treatments. The normative

---

is true, the burden of debt *per se* is relatively small and the question of retirement becomes relatively unimportant.

proposition runs as follows: In allocating the tax burden among individuals, the principle of minimizing the aggregate sacrifice on the whole group should be employed; aggregate sacrifice may be minimized by taxing the rich since the marginal utility of income declines as more income is received.

As applied to debt retirement out of current taxation, this argument would suggest that, in a growing economy in which individual incomes are expected to increase over time, no retirement should take place. Future generations of taxpayers, enjoying a higher income than present taxpayers, can service the debt at a net sacrifice which discounts to a smaller present value than that which would be imposed upon present taxpayers with current redemption of debt.

In its strictest form, this argument requires not only that interpersonal comparisons of utility can be made within a single time period but also that some comparisons can be made between separate time periods. In spite of the fact that the impossibility of making such comparisons in any objective manner has been recognized for a long time, the argument cannot be discarded out of hand. It retains some value if the utilities introduced are conceived to be, not those of the individual taxpayers, but rather those of the individual taxpayers *as they are interpreted by the individual as a decision maker.* If the diminishing marginal utility of income is widely acknowledged, and if social policy based on the assumption of a diminishing marginal utility of income is deemed to be reasonable, the collective choice process may produce results equivalent to those which would have been forthcoming from the assumption of full measurability and comparability.

Although it was not posed in utility terms, the implications of the Domar contribution to debt theory are essentially equivalent to those implicit in the utility argument. Domar showed that the tax rates necessary to service a given public debt must diminish with rising national income. From this the inference is clear that the higher the income the lower the marginal utility of the fixed absolute transfer. He clearly suggests that debt should not be retired. The solution to the debt problem lies not in efforts toward retirement, but in "trying to find ways of achieving a growing national income."[3]

---

3. Evsey D. Domar, "The 'Burden of the Debt' and the National Income," *American Economic Review*, XXXIV (December, 1944). Reprinted in *Readings in Fiscal Policy* (Homewood, Ill., 1955), pp. 479–501, especially p. 500.

Debt Retirement and Economic Growth

The two arguments discussed above tend to support a policy which calls for the servicing of the outstanding public debt of the national government but which makes no positive effort to retire debt. There is a third approach to the problem which leads to the opposite results.

If economic growth is widely accepted, as it seems to be, as a desirable attribute of a well-functioning economic system, public policies aimed at increasing the rate of growth may seem advisable. Implicit in any public action to stimulate growth is the assumption that the rate of growth produced by individual choices within the institutional complex of social, economic, and political forces is less than a "desired" or "optimum" rate. It is, of course, impossible to define an "optimum" growth rate, and it is almost equally difficult to defend the result of private decision making as providing any approach toward an optimum. In setting aside income for savings and in making investment decisions, individuals will tend to adjust their subjective rates of time preference to the rate of return on investment. But the individual schedules of time preference may tend to "underestimate" the value of future income, underestimate being defined in accordance with some indefinable criterion.

Some public action toward stimulating capital formation, an admittedly essential element in rapid economic growth, may be held to be desirable even though the impossibility of determining the "optimum" growth rate is fully acknowledged. There are, of course, many ways in which society could change its public policy in order to stimulate capital formation. Most of these need not concern us here.

One means which is often proposed is that of direct public investment. If this investment (for example, in highways or in river basin development) is debt financed, it will stimulate public capital formation largely at the expense of private capital formation. There will be some net stimulant to economic growth only if the rate of return on the public projects exceeds that which is sacrificed on the private projects which would otherwise have been carried forward. This clarity in conclusion is achieved by begging all the questions concerning the difficulty of defining economic growth in the first place.[4] To

4. Cf. G. Warren Nutter, "On Measuring Economic Growth," *Journal of Political Economy*, LXV (February, 1957), 51–63.

the extent that the proceeds from the sale of public debt instruments are drawn from consumption uses rather than private capital formation, the rate of growth is apparently increased. But it cannot be stated without qualification that a reduction in consumption does not also deter economic growth.

A second scheme is that of financing public investment projects directly from current tax revenues. This will clearly shift the cost to current taxpayers, and it will reduce both the current rate of private consumption as well as private capital formation. Since consumption will be reduced more than in the preceding case, this policy may provide a considerably greater stimulus to economic growth than the financing of similar investment through the medium of loans unless the incentive effects of taxation are overwhelming. There are limitations on any policy of direct public investment, however, in that those areas of economic activity suitable for public investment, and of the type which stimulate economic growth, may be severely restricted.

For a country faced with a large public debt held by private individuals or nonbanking institutions, there exists a third alternative which seems to be preferable in some respects to the two mentioned above. If the community desires collectively to provide a stimulus to more rapid growth, and private capital formation is believed to be important for growth, it can adopt an active policy of debt retirement, financing this retirement out of current tax revenues. This operation will, on the tax side, affect the rate of capital formation only to the same extent as the second alternative mentioned above. And, on the repayment side, a substantial stimulus to new capital formation will be provided. Individuals and institutions securing liquid funds in exchange for government securities will tend to channel a large share of these funds into the market for private securities. Security prices will go up, interest rates will fall, and investment demand will be increased. A relatively small proportion of the liquid funds returned to individuals and institutions in exchange for government securities will be devoted to spending on current consumption items.

This debt retirement method has the advantage of stimulating growth in private capital formation as opposed to public investment. The market can be allowed to serve its normal function in distributing the new investment funds among competing projects in such a way that some approach to an "efficient" utilization is achieved. This means of allocating investment funds does not exist for public investment projects, and competing uses for newly available funds must survive the test imposed by pressure-group political jockeying. There is little assurance that the public investment funds are distributed in accordance with any acceptable criterion of "efficiency."

The suggestion that debt retirement out of current tax revenues provides, in some respects, a superior means of stimulating rapid economic progress does not imply that direct public investment should not be undertaken at the same time. If there exist peculiarly public projects which are closely related to economic development, and which are characterized by underinvestment, direct public outlay is indicated. It has been claimed, for example, that the national investment in an interstate highway network will be highly productive and that such investment will greatly enhance the possibilities of growth in the United States. Any over-all policy program which is directed primarily toward promoting economic growth will probably include some such direct public investment financed preferably out of tax revenues, but also perhaps from new debt issue. The program should also include some debt retirement financed out of current tax revenues. Thus, returning to Domar's argument for a moment, we find that one of the best ways of achieving a growing national income lies in debt retirement.

14. Debt Retirement
and Economic Stabilization

Any fiscal operation which includes debt retirement will tend to exert some effect on prices, income, and employment. The one case in which the effect on these variables does not assume major importance has been discussed in Chapter 13. In all other situations, the important consideration in any policy of debt management must be economic stabilization. Since there are two ways of financing debt retirement, taxation and money creation, it follows that a fiscal operation embodying debt retirement on the one side may serve either to prevent inflation or to prevent deflation or depression. We may first consider anti-inflation measures.

Retirement of Bank-Held Debt

The preceding chapter indicated that a policy of taxation coupled with the retirement of debt held by individuals and nonbanking institutions is, on balance, probably deflationary. But the deflationary impact is not at all certain, and, if present, it is likely to be so slight that a fiscal operation of this sort is not likely to prove suitable for stabilization policy in a period of threatening inflation. When we consider the retirement of public debt held by the banking system, different conclusions follow. We shall first consider the retirement of debt held by the central bank.

Retirement of debt held by the central bank is neither inflationary nor deflationary. The central bank receives money claims for debt instruments. But when the taxation side is taken into account, the combined operation must be deflationary. The deflationary effects of the taxation are not offset by any reflationary effect of the repayment. In a period of threatened inflation, therefore, the levy of taxes to finance the retirement of central bank debt is indicated. The most appropriate means of disposing of a budgetary surplus in such periods is the repurchase of debt instruments held by the Federal Reserve Banks.

For all forms of public debt other than that held by the central bank, the retirement side, taken alone, will tend to be inflationary. As Chapter 11 indicated, debt issue, not debt retirement, is the appropriate anti-inflation measure. Debt held by the central bank does not conform to this rule because it is not pure debt at all. Its retirement does not place additional units of money in the hands of individuals and nonbanking institutions. The retirement process, *per se,* is completely neutral.

Debt held by the commercial banks occupies a position between that held by the central bank and by individuals. The retirement side, taken alone, will increase bank reserves. It will, therefore, be inflationary. Retirement must be financed, however, and when the taxation side is added, the combined process may be deflationary. When taxes are collected, banks must write down demand deposits. When bonds are retired, an asset item is reduced. Reserves are unchanged in the whole operation. Banks can, therefore, expand loans and deposits to the level prevailing prior to the fiscal operation. However, to the extent that the government securities which are retired possess liquidity properties over and above those possessed by other earning assets, banks will not expand deposits back to the previous level. On balance, the operation will tend to be deflationary, although not, of course, equally deflationary with the tax-financed retirement of debt held by the central bank.

Debt Monetization

Debt retirement which is financed by money creation is an appropriate anti-deflation measure. This may be called debt monetization. Debt instruments are replaced by money; liquidity is increased, and spending will be encouraged. In this way the interest cost may be reduced to zero, or at the least to a very nominal figure. In the current institutional setting, effective debt monetization can take place through a retirement of debt held by individuals and institutions and an accompanying sale of debt to the central bank.

Quite clearly this sort of measure represents appropriate policy only when the economy is threatened with, or is characterized by, recession or depression. It will be useful to examine the effects of this operation in some detail.

Just as debt issue to ward off threatened inflation serves to impose some future burden on taxpayers, so debt monetization which prevents deflation removes a burden from the shoulders of future taxpayers. The alternatives to debt retirement in this situation are decreased taxation and increased public spending. Purchasing old government bonds, reducing current tax bills by financing old expenditures, and purchasing new public services are three ways of utilizing newly injected currency, any one of which will accomplish the same real stabilization purpose. The first alternative, monetization of debt, reduces the interest burden on future taxpayers; the other two alternatives largely benefit individuals living at the time of the fiscal operation either in their roles as current taxpayers or as current recipients of public goods and services. The choice among these alternatives must include some consideration of the comparison between present and future benefits.

An example will perhaps help in demonstrating that, even when unemployment exists, the differential beneficiaries of debt monetization are future taxpayers. Assume that an individual holds a government bond worth $100 which may be called by the government. This bond is monetized and the individual receives $100 in currency. With this currency he is able to go into the market and purchase either consumption or investment goods. His net worth is not modified by the debt retirement operation. The bond was valued at its full worth; the transaction shows up on his balance sheet as a simple transformation of assets. Let us assume that he invests the $100 in private securities providing a yield equivalent to that on the government bond which he has given up. In any subsequent income period, the former government bondholder will be in a position identical to that which he would have enjoyed had the debt monetization not taken place. But the individual living in future income periods as a taxpayer will be better off since he will no longer be forced to give up command over real goods and services in order to finance the debt service. The taxpayer is better off through the debt monetization having occurred.

There are, of course, other beneficiaries of the complete operation of which the debt monetization is only a part. The individual's purchase of the private security allows some firm to expand its purchases of investment goods, which in turn increases employment. Individuals owning resources previously unemployed are made better off by the injection of the new purchasing power. But this effect results from the injection of the new money, not from the debt retirement. Again it is necessary to separate the two sides of the process and to analyze the problem in differential terms. The benefits from the injection of new money will be present under any of the three alternatives mentioned. If the new currency (directly issued or secured by "borrowing" from the central bank) is used to finance established public services, allowing current taxes to be reduced, the owners of unemployed resources benefit equally with the situation under debt monetization. The differential beneficiaries in this case are *current* not *future* taxpayers. Similarly with the third alternative; if the new currency is used to finance new public services, the differential beneficiaries are the recipients of these services, whether living presently or in the future.

The extent to which opportunities for substantial debt monetization will present themselves depends upon both the institutional and the behavioral factors in the economy. If the economy should be characterized by the threat of stagnation, as some writers of an earlier period predicted, then opportunities for large-scale debt monetization may exist. However, on the basis of the analysis of the democratic choice process contained in Chapter 12, the hypothesis may be advanced that debt monetization will not normally be chosen over its alternatives. Thus, even in periods of continually threatened recession it seems highly unlikely that significant debt monetization will take place. This conclusion depends, of course, on the implicit assumption that choices among the various stabilization alternatives are made, in the final analysis, in such a way that they are subject to the ordinary pressures inherent in democratic government. If, on the contrary, the choice among these alternatives is not really subjected to the pull and haul of the highly individualized process which we associate with representative government, substantial debt monetization may be accomplished. For example, if a recession threatens to occur, and the Congress should refrain from its natural proclivity to reduce taxes and to expand public spending, the partially independent decision-making authority vested in the Treasury Department and the Federal Reserve Board might monetize a good share of the outstanding national debt. In this case, the analysis of Chapter 12 clearly does not hold since the three alternatives are not really presented to the voter-representative. If, however, Congress should exert its power in the fiscal policy area and act so as to reduce taxes and to increase federal spending, the debt management authorities may not be able to effect any debt monetization even during periods of economic decline. Of course if a deep and long-continued depression should develop, both fiscal policy and debt management policy would be fully appropriate. Significant debt monetization might take place if the 1930's were to be repeated. Indeed the absolute height of folly would be represented by the end of a new depression characterized by more rather than less outstanding debt, measured in some real sense.

If the institutional forces of the economy and the behavior characteristics of individuals are such that neither recession nor inflation should prove to be serious threats, gradual monetization of the national debt can take place as economic growth places new demands on the circulating medium. If the average product price level is to be prevented from falling secularly, some injection of new currency will be needed to finance the expanded flow of real goods and services. One means of injecting this new currency is through debt monetization. Both the tax reduction and the expenditure increase alternatives exist also in this case, but these do not seem so likely to be chosen in this particular setting.

Many competent students think that, at the present time, the forces of the economy are such that inflation represents the underlying tendency, and that stabilization policy over the next few decades will be directed primarily toward countering inflation rather than checking incipient deflation or merely standing neutral with nothing much to do. If this prediction holds true, the chances for substantial debt retirement financed through new currency creation are, for all practical purposes, nonexistent. Debt monetization in this setting would require heroic fiscal policy measures. If inflation is to be prevented, while at the same time debt is to be monetized, increased taxation and reduced spending must do double duty. Not only must fiscal policy, through the generation of budgetary surpluses, be sufficient to offset the natural tendencies of the economy toward inflation, but it must also offset the inflationary effects deliberately fostered by the monetization of debt.

A far more likely prospect is that some unintended debt retirement will be accomplished through inflation itself. One of the distributional gainers from inflation is the future taxpayer obligated to finance the fixed service charge on the national debt. Inflation can all but wipe out the real weight of the debt. This is accomplished, in large part, by the simple dispossession of the bondholder.

If inflation is to be avoided, recent experience indicates that reliance must be placed on monetary policy. While the effects of central bank policy to increase interest rates may be to reduce the real value of outstanding debt instruments, when refunding takes place, additional debt, in real terms, must be created unless the Treasury policy is to run counter to that of the central bank. In many respects, as suggested in Chapter 11, fiscal policy measures would be more appropriate, more efficient, and perhaps to some, more equitable. But democratic governments do not seem to impose direct taxes upon the people solely to prevent the hidden taxes of inflation. So long as the quasi-independent monetary authorities can accomplish the same purpose through monetary policy, perhaps the additional burden thereby placed on future taxpayers is not too high a price to pay for stability. An entirely acceptable solution to the problem of economic stabilization is not likely to be achieved until and unless there are incorporated into the institutional structure some clearly defined and predictable rules for policy. Inflation does not represent a proper alternative to be placed before individuals who must make decisions on economic policy, whether they be voters, representatives, or administrators. Society should not be forced to decide on the question as to how much economic stability it desires. Economic stability should be a predictable outcome of the rules of the system, rules which are constructed once and for all, and which are, in a real sense, relatively absolute absolutes.

Appendix
A Suggested Conceptual Revaluation
of the National Debt

I. Introduction

This Appendix represents an attempt to apply the theory of public debt contained in the earlier chapters to the general problem of measuring the magnitude or size of the national debt. It is an exploratory effort designed to raise and to isolate the relevant issues rather than to resolve all of the complexities which may appear. With this quite limited objective in view, I have not tried to provide definitive solutions to the measurement problem. Insofar as the argument requires, I have used actual data on the national debt for illustrative purposes. But I should emphasize the illustrative usage as opposed to any presumed factual presentation or rearrangement of data.

II. The General Measurement Problem as Applied to Private Debt

Public debt has traditionally been measured in terms of the principal or maturity value, that is, the amount which must be repaid at the maturity date, and, except for securities issued at a discount, the amount of funds transferred to the government when the debt is created.[1] This apparently simple measurement has its origin in the treatment of private debt. Since the prin-

---

1. All of the national debt of the United States is measured in this way except for Savings Bonds which are carried in the debt totals at current redemption values. For these securities the additional debt which accrues through time shows up also as expenditure, presumably in the interest item of the budget.

cipal represents the payment necessary to discharge fully the obligation of the debt, it seems appropriate that this be used in measuring debt size. The implications of this measurement procedure do not seem to have been thoroughly examined.

Let us initially suppose that a riskless private loan is contracted and that the structure of interest rates remains stable through time. The interest rate paid on this loan will be a "pure" rate unalloyed by any risk premium. Competition will insure that this rate approximates that paid on other riskless loans in the economy. Under these circumstances there can be no question but that the size of the debt is best shown by the maturity value. This indicates the value of an alternative capital asset of identical risk characteristics which would be required to provide a yield sufficient to cover fully the debt obligation. In a slightly different sense, the maturity value also represents the capitalized value of the future payments stream if this stream is capitalized at the pure rate of yield on investment. In this particular example, the stream of payments is capitalized at the internal rate, obviously yielding the maturity value as a capitalized sum.

Let us now introduce a second model in which a private loan of some riskiness is contracted. We shall continue to assume that the structure of interest rates remains stable over time. In this case, the interest rate paid must include some risk premium; it must exceed that paid on the no-risk investment. The maturity value of the debt will not be equal to the capitalized value of the stream of payments, capitalized at the pure rate of yield. For example, suppose that we are considering a loan of $100 (which we may convert to a loan in perpetuity by the assumption of refunding at the same rate) at an interest rate of 10 per cent while the pure rate of yield is 5 per cent. The capitalization of a $10-payments stream in perpetuity yields a total value of $200. The debt claim will, however, be worth only $100 in the market. In other words, $100 will be sufficient to purchase an asset of equivalent risk characteristics. The $100 purchase will not, of course, provide a certain yield which will guarantee that the initial debt can be fully serviced. If the borrower desires a perfect hedge against the debt, he must purchase that asset which will yield the $10 with certainty. This asset will command a market price of $200. But this $200 asset will more than remove the debt obligation represented by the original loan. It will also remove from either borrower or lender the risk which the lender assumed in the original transaction. The purchase of the $100 asset is sufficient to place both borrower and lender in a position identical to that which they enjoyed prior to the debt transaction.

The measure of the size of private debt in terms of maturity values is less appropriate when the assumption of stability in the structure of interest rates is dropped. If the pure rate of yield on private investment changes subsequent to the contraction of a private loan, the capitalization process suggested above will yield a different value for debt than the principal or maturity value. And, for many purposes, this capital value is more useful in indicating the real weight of the debt. Suppose, to return to our first model, that a riskless loan of $100 is contracted at the pure rate of 5 per cent. Subsequently, the rate of yield on marginal investments in the economy falls to 4 per cent. The capitalization process now yields $125 as a measure of the debt rather than $100. This indicates that the full discharge of the debt obligation is now equivalent to the sacrifice of an alternative earning asset commanding a price of $125. The larger figure is obviously more appropriate as a measure if the debt instrument is marketable; but, when considered correctly, it is equally appropriate when debt instruments are not marketable.

III. Measuring Local Government Debt

The maturity value measure is applicable only in a more restricted sense to local government debt. Initially, let us assume once again that the structure of interest rates does not change over time. In this case, as with private debt, the maturity value of the debt will represent the market value of resources which must be sacrificed in order to finance the purchase of a capital asset of characteristics identical to the debt obligation. But the special feature of local government debt is that income from local government securities is tax exempt. This means that such securities may be marketed at a rate which is lower than the pure rate of yield on marginal investment in the private sector. The effects of this feature on the measurement problem must be examined.

Again it will be helpful to consider a simplified numerical example. Suppose that some local government issues a bond for $100 at a rate of 3 per cent while the pure rate of yield on private investment is 4 per cent. Again we shall assume that the maturing issues are continually refunded, allowing the fixed maturity security to be converted conceptually into a security of no maturity date. The $3 annual interest payment discounts to a value of only $75 when this payments stream is capitalized at the pure yield rate. But the market will operate so as to insure that an equivalent asset commands a market price of $100. The local unit of government may, if it desires, purchase a no-risk asset for $75 which will yield an income sufficient to service the debt. This suggests that the $75 provides a more useful measure for the size of the debt than the $100 maturity value or, in the case of the no-maturity security, the principal.

Actually, however, both the $75 and the $100 measure must be used. It is true that a tax payment of only $75 would be required to offset the debt. But the discharge of the debt will also eliminate from the economy a tax exemption which has a capital value of $25 under our assumptions. Therefore, the market value of resources which must be given up, in present or future periods, by individuals in order to discharge fully the obligation represented by the debt is $100. The maturity value measure is the more useful one when the problem is considered in this light. However, when it is recognized that the local taxpaying group may be quite different from the bond purchasing group, the measure becomes less useful. The bonds issued by single local units of government are normally marketed nationally. The advantages of the tax exemption feature are secured by federal taxpayers scattered throughout the economy. The capital value of the tax exemption is held, not by local taxpayers of the borrowing jurisdiction, but by bond purchasers from the entire nation. Therefore, it is not proper to attribute to local taxpayers the supplementary capital value of the tax exemption. The $75 figure more correctly measures the size of local government debt when the single local unit of government is considered in isolation.[2]

---

2. This is not the place to introduce an extended discussion of local government financing. But the above example does illustrate quite clearly how a local unit of government may (if its charter allows) finance expenditures without imposing any cost upon its own taxpayers, either present or future. Let us suppose that a local unit decides to construct a school building at a cost of $1 million. To finance this building, it issues bonds totaling $4 million at 3 per cent. It then devotes $1 million of the proceeds to the actual construction of the school. With the remaining $3 million it enters the private securities market and purchases assets which provide a pure yield of 4 per cent. These assets provide a sufficient income to enable the service charges on the local government debt to be fully offset. Local taxpayers are freed from any burden of payment when the school building is constructed, and they are not obligated to pay taxes to service the local debt. The cost of

On the other hand, when aggregate local debt is considered, the use of maturity values seems necessary. Those individuals holding the bonds of any one jurisdiction must be taxpayers in some local unit, and, therefore, the capital value of the tax exemption must be added in when all local debts are taken into account.

Just as in the case of private debt, when the assumption of stability in the interest rate structure is dropped, the use of principal to measure debt size is not acceptable, even in the measurement of aggregate local government debt. If interest rates increase after the sale of local securities, the borrowing jurisdiction may, if it chooses, repurchase its own securities for a price below that indicated by the principal of the loan. The size of the aggregate local government debt at any moment in time seems to be best measured by the amount of current tax collections which would be required to finance the purchase of an earning asset which will yield an income sufficient to service all outstanding debt plus the capital value of the tax exemption feature. To return to the numerical example, let us suppose that the pure rate of yield on marginal investment increases from 4 per cent to 5 per cent subsequent to the debt issue. The capitalization process yields a sum of $60 instead of $75 as the amount of taxes required to purchase an earning asset yielding a sum sufficient to service the debt. If the local unit is considered in isolation, this becomes the measure of the debt. If, on the other hand, the aggregate local debt is to be measured, the capital value of the tax exemption feature must also be calculated. The differential yield of $1 capitalized at 5 per cent rather than 4

---

the project is shifted to federal government taxpayers in general and local citizens pay only in their capacities as federal taxpayers.

In such a situation, the local government is merely taking advantage of an opportunity to make a profit through arbitrage. The differential between the rate of yield on municipals and on private bonds is, of course, exaggerated in the example. But so long as any differential at all exists, the operation outlined here is possible.

Local units of government are normally prevented by charter from investing in private securities. They may be allowed, however, to invest in federal government securities. And here, too, if a differential in rate should be present, local taxpayers can be relieved of a large portion of their normal public expenditure burden through a similar operation.

The implication of this appears to be that, if federal income tax rates should remain high, the stiffening of debt limit laws restricting local government borrowing or the removal of all investing opportunities may prove desirable.

per cent gives a total capital value of $20 rather than $25. When aggregate local debt is measured, the appropriate magnitude now becomes $80 instead of $100.

IV. The National Debt

The two preceding sections have shown that the normally accepted measurement procedures may not provide meaningful totals for private debt and for local government debt under certain conditions. The use of principal or maturity value to measure the magnitude of the debt obligation is even less applicable for the national debt. The fundamental reason for the difference lies, of course, in the possession of money-creating powers by the central or national government. As earlier chapters have shown, the existence of this power, along with that of pure debt creation, has led to some confusion. In the discussion which follows I shall propose an alternative way of evaluating the debt, at least conceptually, which should be of some assistance in clarifying the distinction between real or pure debt and monetized debt.

How large is the national debt? As of July 31, 1957, official records indicate that the national debt of the United States amounted to $272.5 billion. What does this figure tell us? This is somewhat more difficult to answer. It may provide some information concerning the amount of purchasing power which was transferred to government at some time in the past by individuals and institutions. There is, however, no way of knowing whether or not this purchasing power was actually transferred *away* from the private economy. All, none, or any portion of this purchasing power may have been *created* in the process of debt issue. The $272.5 billion figure tells us nothing about the real debt which was created, nor does it tell us anything about the amount of real resources which must currently be given up if we choose to discharge fully the debt obligation.

The confusion generated by the use of this measure may be readily illustrated by frequently encountered popular statements which claim that each man, woman, and child in the United States owes a national debt of some $1,600. This is computed by dividing the debt total of $272 billion by some current estimate for population. From this the inference is often drawn, implicitly or explicitly, that the full discharge of the debt obligation would require that additional current taxes in the amount of $1,600 be levied on each individual (on the average).

If we neglect for the time being the fact that interest rates have risen sharply since the issue of large portions of the national debt, the inference would seem valid in terms of the analogy with private debt. When the adjustment to present market values is made (an adjustment which applies equally to private and public debt), such a per capita computation should indicate the market value of real resources which each individual would have to sacrifice to discharge fully his per capita share of the national debt obligation.

It is obvious, however, that the inference is almost wholly incorrect when applied to national debt. Here the analogy between public and private debt appears to be false. The explanation is not difficult to find. A large part of the national debt does not represent pure debt at all. This part is essentially "money" both when issued and as held by individuals and institutions. This being the case, full tax financing of debt retirement would act to destroy "money" in the system, thereby generating serious destabilizing effects. The analogy breaks down here only because of this mixture of pure debt and "money" in what we normally refer to as national debt. As the analysis of this book has demonstrated, the analogy fully holds when pure or real debt is considered. Quite obviously money is not debt.

Any meaningful measure of the national debt should reflect the same information as that which is provided by the accepted measure of private debt. That is, this measure should indicate the capital value of resources which must be given up or sacrificed in order to discharge fully the debt obligation. It should indicate the total tax collection, in real terms, which is required to retire all national debt without, at the same time, exerting significant over-all effects on the absolute price level. In other words, the conceptual retirement operation should be neutral in its effects on the level of economic activity. If the use of maturity values as adjusted to take account of changes in interest rates fails this test, how may such a meaningful measure be constructed?

The solution is to be found in the capitalization process discussed above for private debt and local government debt. If the interest payments stream is capitalized at a rate indicating the pure rate of yield on marginal investments in the private sector, the resultant capital value will provide an accurate measure of the national debt in some meaningful sense. This approach was shown to be faulty in application to private debt and to local government debt in the aggregative sense. The capital value, calculated in this manner, was shown to diverge from the principal of the debt in the one case because of the failure to include a differential risk premium and in the other because of its omission of a differential tax exemption feature. But the market appropriately places some values, negative or positive, on these features. And the private individual is forced to abide by market evaluations in purchasing equivalent assets or in repurchasing debt instruments.

In the case of the national debt, however, the measure yielded by the capitalization process suggested is much more useful. Quite clearly, as Section V will demonstrate, the current interest charges capitalized at an estimated rate for the net or pure yield on capital investment will provide a figure far below either the maturity value of the national debt or for this latter value adjusted downward for the recent increases in the level of interest rates. It is equally clear that this difference is primarily due to the fact that the national debt instruments possess many characteristics of money. This being true, the adjusted maturity value does not reflect the value of real resources which would have to be given up to discharge the debt.

Money may be issued at zero cost. Therefore, that portion of the national debt which does represent "money" in its relevance to human behavior can be replaced with actual money, currency, without private people being forced to sacrifice real goods and services. The share of total debt, as measured, which represents genuine or pure debt can best be determined from the capitalization process suggested.

In the following section I shall attempt to apply this proposed measurement process to the national debt of the United States.

V. How Large Is the National Debt?

As of July 31, 1957, the national debt, as measured, amounted to $272.5 billion. This may be called, for our purposes, the principal or the maturity value measure. Since interest rates have risen since much of the debt has been issued, the first step in any evaluation is that of adjusting this value downward to reflect the reduction in capital value which has taken place. The government debt may be conceptually repurchased for less than the principal sum outstanding.

An extremely rough calculation suggests that the adjusted market value of national debt as of July 31, 1957, was $257 billion.[3] This figure represents the cash outlay which will enable the government conceptually to repurchase all outstanding debt, either directly through established markets or indirectly through "hedging" sale and repurchase of additional debt sufficient to offset nonmarketable issues.[4]

There are two means through which the necessary cash outlay of $257 billion may be secured. Money may be printed directly, or taxes may be levied. The $257 billion figure tells us nothing concerning the breakdown between these two sources. To secure such a breakdown, the capitalization process suggested above must be introduced.

The annual interest charge on the national debt as of July, 1957, is estimated at $7.4 billion. This amounts to 2.7 per cent of the maturity value of $272.5 billion, and almost 2.9 per cent of the adjusted market value of $257 billion. Quite clearly neither of these represents an appropriate capitalization rate in the 1950's. This rate should be representative of the pure rate of yield on capital investment at the margin of use. Without making any detailed at-

3. The calculation is direct for marketable securities. The government could repurchase these below par. For nonmarketable issues, this sort of repurchase alternative is not open, but the government may, conceptually, convert this nonmarketable debt to marketable debt by selling marketable securities at current prices sufficient to offset fully the service and the amortization of the nonmarketable issues. To estimate the appropriate capital value of the marketable securities which would have to be sold in such an operation, some present market value must be applied to the nonmarketable securities. In the calculation here I have used the same market-to-maturity value ratio as that found to apply for the whole of the marketable debt. I have applied this ratio to all nonmarketable securities, including securities held by governmental trust funds, except Savings Bonds which are already carried in debt totals at current redemption values.

All data employed in making this calculation were taken from *Treasury Bulletin* for September, 1957.

4. It is important to emphasize the conceptual nature of this repurchase operation. If the government *actually* attempts to repurchase its own securities, prices will be driven up and current market values will provide no measure of the actual money cost of retiring all debt. It does not seem appropriate, however, to include this adjustment in the calculations made. The aim is that of deriving some measure which will be useful in indicating the weight of carrying the debt, a measure which is in capital-value dimensions. Whether or not an actual repurchase operation would exert significant effects on bond prices will depend on the source of the funds and also upon the degree of substitution between government bonds and private bonds. See Footnote 6 for further discussion.

tempt to determine this rate accurately, I shall make the assumption that this rate is 4 per cent.[5] If the $7.4 billion (assumed to be the value of the interest payments stream in perpetuity) is capitalized at a 4 per cent rate, we get a capital value of $185 billion, not $257 billion. This figure comes much closer to providing a measure of national debt in some "pure" sense. By the current sacrifice of $185 billion in privately owned earning assets or in consumption goods, the national debt can be fully retired, provided we can neglect the possible secondary effects of the retirement process itself on the structure of interest rates.[6] A more direct statement can be made in a slightly different manner. The net yield from $185 billion of earning assets in the private economy is obligated to the service of the national debt.

The remaining $72 billion represent that portion of the national debt which is, for the most part, "money" in its relevance to human behavior.[7] This suggests that, secondary effects aside, the national debt could be wiped off the books with a capital levy of $185 billion and a direct currency creation of $72 billion. The additional currency would be needed to offset the deflationary impact of the debt retirement, and to keep the whole operation "neutral" in its stabilization effects. Having removed the debt instruments, possessing much "moneyness," there would have to be more nominal units of money introduced in order to prevent serious deflationary consequences. But this

5. This is based on the average yield for July, 1957, on Moody's AAA Corporation Bonds.

6. These secondary effects may be easily exaggerated. The conceptual refunding operation proposed would change interest rates only insofar as the tax imposed to finance the pure debt retirement reduces consumption spending more than the retirement itself increases consumption spending. Since some effect in this direction seems probable, the whole operation will tend to reduce interest rates and to increase the capitalized value of real debt. This complication may be avoided by assuming that the capitalization rate used is some average of the initial pure rate of yield and that rate which would prevail after the conceptual refunding. The difference between these two rates would depend on the size of the debt and on the elasticity of demand for private investment funds.

7. This differential may, in part, represent other features. For example, if "patriotism" should cause individuals to accept a lower rate on public than on private loans, the capital value of this feature would be included in the $72 billion. This, and other "nonmoneyness" features, might create some difficulties if the conceptual refunding discussed were to be actually attempted since these features could not be replaced by currency. Their introduction does not, however, change the appropriateness of measuring real or pure debt by the $185 billion. In the text, we assume that the differential is represented by "moneyness" alone.

additional money needed may be created without cost, and, therefore, it should not be included in any estimate of "pure" debt.

It is to be emphasized that I am proposing a conceptual revaluation of the debt, not any actual attempt at retirement. Specifically, what is suggested is that the manner of measuring the debt be modified and that an additional and supplementary evaluation be made. The total process of debt measurement should look as follows:

National Debt as of July, 1957

		Billions of Dollars
1. National debt, maturity value		$272
2. National debt, present market value		257
3. National debt, "pure"	$185	
National debt, "monetized"	72	
	$257	

This account would be useful in many respects. First of all, it would indicate more accurately the real burden of debt which is being shifted forward to future generations of taxpayers. This is the $185 billion, not the $257 or the $275 billion. The burden of the $72 billion, if it existed, was not a burden of pure debt *but of inflation,* and, as such, *has already been shouldered.* Future generations will be little affected by this portion of the nominal debt. Similar conclusions follow for the $18 billion difference between the maturity value and the present market value. This no longer exists as a debt obligation; this portion has been "retired" through the levy of a "tax" on the holders of government securities.

VI. Treasury Refunding Operations

One of the most important uses of this supplementary account would be that of providing an accurate check on the effects of Treasury refunding operations. Suppose that the Treasury succeeds in refunding a portion of the debt at a lower rate of interest. This is accomplished, assuming that the general pattern of rates is not changing, by replacing debt instruments possessing less "moneyness" with debt instruments possessing more "moneyness." Let us assume that a particular operation of this sort reduces the annual interest charge from $7.4 to $7 billion. We shall continue to assume that the pure rate of yield is 4 per cent. This operation reduces the value of pure debt from $185 to $175 billion, while the value of the monetized debt is increased by $10 billion. In this way it becomes obvious that the refunding operation is equivalent to the retirement of pure debt. Future generations of taxpayers are relieved of an annual interest charge of $.4 billion, and individuals living currently are subjected to a possible burden of an additional $10 billion. In the full-employment setting, a refunding of this sort will be inflationary, and the $10 billion may be considered a tax on the holders of cash balances and government securities. The refunding will have shifted a real burden of debt from future taxpayers to these groups. If unemployment should be present, the inflationary consequences need not occur. And here the burden may be removed from future taxpayers without placing substantial real cost on individuals currently living. Under these conditions, this type of refunding is, of course, to be recommended.

The opposing case may now be considered. We assume that the Treasury succeeds in increasing the total interest charge on the debt. This is accomplished by replacing debt instruments possessing considerable "moneyness" with others which more closely resemble pure debt. Again for purposes of illustration, suppose that a particular operation increases the annual interest charge from $7.4 to $7.8 billion. This will increase the value of pure debt from $185 billion to $195 billion, assuming the same capitalization rate of 4 per cent. The operation is equivalent to the issue of $10 billion additional pure debt. The monetized debt is reduced by $10 billion.

This operation will be deflationary, at least relative to what would have taken place in its absence. But the deflation itself must relieve present taxpayers at the expense of future taxpayers in this case. The government secures no greater share of resources than before the refunding; but it agrees to pay more future income than before. Individuals, after the operation, hold more claims to future income. The net value of claims to current income ("money") and to future income (pure debt) has not been modified. But claims to current income have been reduced and claims to future income increased. Those who give up the claims to current incomes in exchange for greater claims on future incomes are not harmed by the operation. They are purchasing pure debt instruments. On the other hand, those who are unaffected directly by the operation gain by the deflation imposed, assuming that we may neglect distributional consequences.

This analysis may be clarified somewhat by a more specific example. Suppose that Individual A holds, prior to the refunding, a security with a maturity value of $100 yielding only 3 per cent interest because of specific redemption features which allow this security to fill a near-money role in his portfolio. The Treasury offers him in exchange a $100 security which yields 4 per cent but which does not carry with it these "moneyness" features. The individual accepts the offer and the exchange is made. Clearly, future taxpayers are charged with the additional $1 of interest. Individual A will find it necessary to reduce his rate of spending on current real goods and services sufficiently to restore his liquidity position. He will find it necessary to withdraw approximately $25 from circulation. The goods and services so released will become available to the whole social group. Other individuals will be benefited by the refunding while Individual A will have undergone merely a transformation of his assets. In this simple model, the net effect on the current generation must be beneficial.

The conclusions reached on such a simple model must be modified if we introduce leverage effects stemming from fractional reserve banking. For example, if the refunding operation should take the form of retiring debt held by the central bank and replacing it with debt held by individuals, the reduction in liquidity occasioned by the retirement may be some multiple of the actual maturity value of the debt involved. In this case the refunding operation has the effect of removing "powerful" money from the system and replacing it with "weak" money. Whether or not this is desirable will depend on the stage of the cycle in which the refunding operation takes place. Refunding at higher yields is equivalent to borrowing solely to prevent inflation. This case was analyzed somewhat more fully in Chapter 11.

The analysis to this point has assumed that the level or pattern of interest rates does not change with any Treasury refunding. But clearly interest rates do change, and this must now be taken into account. Let us return to the first example in which the total interest charge is reduced from $7.4 to $7 billion. In saying that this operation reduces pure debt from $185 to $175 billion, the old rate of 4 per cent for the net yield on private investment was employed. But a refunding of this magnitude would tend to reduce the level of interest rates, and thus the appropriate capitalization rate. And if the annual interest payments stream is reduced, but at the same time the capitalization rate is reduced, will the amount of pure debt, as calculated in the manner proposed, necessarily be changed? It may readily be demonstrated that the amount of pure debt must also be reduced under these conditions, although by less than in the previous example. It is true that the operation may reduce both the interest payment and the appropriate rate of capitalization. But it is impossible for the Treasury operation alone to reduce the rate of capitalization, defined as the estimated net yield on zero-risk investment *in the whole economy*, proportionately with the interest payment. The interest charge is calculated for the national debt alone; the rate of capitalization is taken from the whole economy. The refunding operation must, therefore, effect an increase in monetized debt and a decrease in real debt.

Similar conclusions follow when the opposite sort of refunding is considered. Here the general level of interest rates will tend to increase, and thus the appropriate discount rate. But this rate cannot increase proportionately with the interest charge. Pure debt must increase and monetized debt decrease.

The necessity for taking the change in the rate of capitalization into account along with the change in the payments stream need not make the conceptual revaluation much more difficult. Since the purpose is that of allowing us to define somewhat more specifically the effects of a refunding operation, the revaluation can be conducted in an *ex poste* sense, that is, after both the payments stream and the capitalization rate have maintained their newer levels.

VII. Relation with Simons' Proposal

Henry Simons, in his famous paper on debt policy,[8] suggested that all of the national debt should be refunded into consols or transformed into currency. The revaluation proposed here is a means of accomplishing the purpose desired by Simons without necessarily undertaking the drastic steps which he suggested. The revaluation proposal is based on an acceptance of the fact that the public debt instruments, as issued, will continue to fall anywhere

8. Henry Simons, "On Debt Policy," *Journal of Political Economy*, LII (December, 1944), 356–61. Reprinted in *Economic Policy for a Free Society* (Chicago, 1948), pp. 222–30.

along the spectrum between currency and consols, or more properly put, between currency and pure debt instruments.[9] The revaluation serves to separate these two aspects of the national debt. In a sense it represents a conceptual refunding along the lines which Simons suggested. By revaluing debt through the capitalization of the annual interest charge on the basis of the net yield on no-risk investment, we are essentially isolating that portion of the debt which can be refunded as consols, that form of debt as far removed from currency as is possible. The remainder (subtracting the first item from present market rather than maturity value) can be considered as being refunded into currency. This step alone will clarify discussion of the debt, and it would seem to be relatively less important whether or not an actual refunding along these lines takes place. The confusion which has been based on the fact that actual debt instruments possess features of both currency and pure debt would be substantially eliminated by reference to the account proposed.

9. Consols themselves, insofar as they possess some "moneyness," do not represent pure debt in the full sense of the term as here discussed. But since consols do approach pure debt instruments closely, we may, for present purposes, largely disregard the difference.

Indexes

Index of Authors

Index of Subjects

This book is set in Minion, a typeface designed by Robert Slimbach specifically for digital typesetting. Released by Adobe in 1989, it is a versatile neohumanist face that shows the influence of Slimbach's own calligraphy.

This book is printed on paper that is acid-free and meets the requirements of the American National Standard for Permanence of Paper for Printed Library Materials, z39.48-1992. ♾

Book design by Louise OFarrell, Gainesville, Fla.
Typography by Impressions Book and Journal Services, Inc., Madison, Wisc.
Printed and bound by Edwards Brothers, Inc., Ann Arbor, Mich.